THE BROTHERS KARAMAZOV

Fyodor Dostoevsky

INTRODUCTION:
STOPPING TO BUY SPARKNOTES ON A SNOWY EVENING

Whose words these are you *think* you know.
Your paper's due tomorrow, though;
We're glad to see you stopping here
To get some help before you go.

Lost your course? You'll find it here.
Face tests and essays without fear.
Between the words, good grades at stake:
Get great results throughout the year.

Once school bells caused your heart to quake
As teachers circled each mistake.
Use SparkNotes and no longer weep,
Ace every single test you take.

Yes, books are lovely, dark, and deep,
But only what you grasp you keep,
With hours to go before you sleep,
With hours to go before you sleep.

CONTENTS

CONTEXT

FYODOR DOSTOEVSKY IS RENOWNED as one of the world's greatest novelists and literary psychologists. Born in Moscow in 1821, the son of a doctor, Dostoevsky was educated first at home and then at a boarding school. When Dostoevsky was a young boy, his father sent him to the St. Petersburg Academy of Military Engineering, from which he graduated in 1843. Dostoevsky had long been interested in writing, and he immediately resigned from his position as a sublieutenant to devote his time to his craft. His first book, *Poor Folk* (1846), was immediately popular with critics.

Dostoevsky's early view of the world was shaped by his experience of social injustice. At the age of twenty-six, Dostoevsky became active in socialist circles, largely because of his opposition to the institution of serfdom. His political opinions were influenced by his experiences as a young boy—his father was murdered by his own serfs while Dostoevsky was away at school. Another experience that greatly affected Dostoevsky, and that found its way into his writing, was the time he spent in prison. On April 23, 1849, Dostoevsky was arrested for his participation in a group that illegally printed and distributed socialist propaganda. After spending eight months in prison, Dostoevsky was sentenced to death for membership in the group and was led, with other members of the group, to be shot. But the execution turned out to be a mere show, meant to punish the prisoners psychologically. Dostoevsky then spent four years at a labor camp in Siberia, followed by four years of military service. Raskolnikov's time in a Siberian prison, described in the Epilogue of *Crime and Punishment,* is based on Dostoevsky's own experiences at a similar prison, and he devoted many passages in his other books to scenes involving criminal justice, including the courtroom scenes of *The Brothers Karamazov.*

Dostoevsky's time in prison affected him in at least two important ways. First, during his imprisonment Dostoevsky began suffering from epileptic seizures, a condition from which he suffered for the rest of his life. He portrays the experience of epilepsy through the character of Smerdyakov in *The Brothers Karamazov.* The second important change that Dostoevsky underwent in prison was his rejection of the radical socialist positions that had led to his arrest, and his development of a conservative concern for traditional values. His conservative religious and philosophical inclination is evident throughout his works written after this period, including *The Brother's Karamazov.* For instance, Dostoevsky specifically questions whether good and evil can exist in a world in which there is no God. Through the character of Rakitin, Dostoevsky parodies the progressive theories of his contemporaries, intellectuals who move from popular idea to popular idea according to the whims of fashion, without regard for the truth.

In 1857, Dostoevsky married Mariya Dmitriyevna Isayeva, who died of consumption seven years later. He spent much of the 1860s in Western Europe, experiencing the culture that was slowly invading Russia. During this time he struggled with poverty, epilepsy, and an addiction to gambling. But with the publication of *Crime and Punishment* (1866), his fortunes improved. The novel's popular and critical success allowed him to keep ahead, albeit just barely, of daunting debts and the burden of supporting a number of children left in his care after the deaths of his brother and sister. In 1867, he married a second time, to Anna Grigoryevna Snitkina, who helped him cope with his epilepsy, depression, and gambling problems. Anna had served as his stenographer for his novel *The Gambler* (1867).

After writing *Crime and Punishment,* Dostoevsky wrote *The Idiot* (1868), and perhaps his greatest masterwork, *The Brothers Karamazov* (1880). *The Brothers Karamazov* is Dostoevsky's deepest and most complex examination of crucial philosophical questions of human existence. In it, he addresses the conflict between faith and doubt, the problem of free will, and the question of moral responsibility. *The Brothers Karamazov* is one of the greatest novels of the nineteenth century, and remains the capstone of Dostoevsky's achievement today. Dostoevsky died in 1881, only a year after *The Brothers Karamazov* was published.

Some people have seen Dostoevsky's novels as prophetic depictions of life under the Soviet regime. The existentialist movement that took shape in the middle of the twentieth century looked to him for his descriptions of human beings confronting mortality, despair, and the anxiety of choice. Writers such as Albert Camus and Jean-Paul Sartre valued Dostoevsky's writing for his profound insights into human dilemmas, which, along with his style, themes, and unforgettable characters, continue to influence writers more than a century after his death.

PLOT OVERVIEW

I
N HIS YOUTH, Fyodor Pavlovich Karamazov is a coarse, vulgar
man whose main concerns are making money and seducing
young women. He marries twice and has three sons: Dmitri, the
child of his first wife, and Ivan and Alyosha, children of his second wife. Fyodor Pavlovich never has any interest in his sons,
and when their mothers die, he sends them away to be brought up by
relatives and friends. At the beginning of the novel, Dmitri Karamazov, who is now a twenty-eight-year-old soldier, has just returned
to Fyodor Pavlovich's town. Fyodor Pavlovich is unhappy to see
Dmitri because Dmitri has come to claim an inheritance left to him
by his mother. Fyodor Pavlovich plans to keep the inheritance for
himself. The two men swiftly fall into conflict over the money, and the
coldly intellectual Ivan, who knows neither his father nor his brother
well, is eventually called in to help settle their dispute. The kind, faithful
Alyosha, who is about twenty, also lives in the town, where he is an aco-
lyte, or apprentice, at the monastery, studying with the renowned elder
Zosima. Eventually Dmitri and Fyodor Pavlovich agree that perhaps
Zosima could help resolve the Karamazovs' quarrel, and Alyosha tentatively consents to arrange a meeting.

At the monastery, Alyosha's worst fears are realized. After Fyodor Pavlovich makes a fool of himself by mocking the monks and
telling vulgar stories, Dmitri arrives late, and Dmitri and Fyodor
Pavlovich become embroiled in a shouting match. It turns out that
they have more to quarrel about than money: they are both in love
with Grushenka, a beautiful young woman in the town. Dmitri has
left his fiancée, Katerina, to pursue Grushenka, while Fyodor Pavlovich has promised to give Grushenka 3,000 rubles if she becomes
his lover. This sum is significant, as Dmitri recently stole 3,000 rubles
from Katerina in order to finance a lavish trip with Grushenka, and he
is now desperate to pay the money back. As father and son shout at
each other at the monastery, the wise old Zosima unexpectedly kneels
and bows his head to the ground at Dmitri's feet. He later explains to
Alyosha that he could see that Dmitri is destined to suffer greatly.

Many years previously, Fyodor Pavlovich Karamazov fathered a
fourth son with a retarded mute girl who lived in town as the village
idiot. The girl died as she gave birth to the baby, who was taken in by
servants of Fyodor Pavlovich and forced to work as a servant for

him as well. Fyodor Pavlovich never treats the child, Smerdyakov, as a son, and Smerdyakov develops a strange and malicious personality. He also suffers from epilepsy. Despite the limitations of his upbringing, however, Smerdyakov is not stupid. He enjoys nothing more than listening to Ivan discuss philosophy, and in his own conversations, he frequently invokes many of Ivan's ideas—specifically that the soul is not immortal, and that therefore morality does not exist and the categories of good and evil are irrelevant to human experience.

After the humiliating scene in the monastery, the rest of Alyosha's day is only slightly less trying. Dmitri sends Alyosha to break off Dmitri's engagement with Katerina. Alyosha then argues about religion with Ivan in front of the smirking Fyodor Pavlovich. Alyosha also gets caught in the middle of another explosion between Dmitri and Fyodor Pavlovich over Grushenka, in the course of which Dmitri throws Fyodor Pavlovich to the ground and threatens to kill him. But despite the hardships of his day, Alyosha is so gentle and loving that he is concerned only with how he might help his family. After tending his father's wounds, he returns to the monastery for the night.

The next day, Alyosha visits Katerina. To his surprise, Ivan is with Katerina, and Alyosha immediately perceives that Ivan and Katerina are in love. Alyosha tries to convince them that they should act on their love for one another, but they are both too proud and cold to listen. Alyosha has dinner with Ivan, and Ivan explains to him the source of his religious doubt: he cannot reconcile the idea of a loving God with the needless suffering of innocent people, particularly children. Any God that would allow such suffering, he says, does not love mankind. He recites a poem he has written called "The Grand Inquisitor," in which he accuses Christ of placing an intolerable burden upon humanity by guaranteeing that people have free will and the ability to choose whether or not to believe in God.

That evening, Alyosha again returns to the monastery, where the frail Zosima is now on his deathbed. Alyosha hurries to Zosima's cell, and arrives just in time to hear his final lesson, which emphasizes the importance of love and forgiveness in all human affairs. Zosima dies stretching his arms out before him, as though to embrace the world.

Many of the monks are optimistic that Zosima's death will be accompanied by a miracle, but no miracle takes place. If anything, Zosima's corpse begins to stink more quickly than might have been expected, which is taken by Zosima's critics to mean that he was corrupt and unreliable in life. Sickened by the injustice of seeing the wise and loving Zosima humiliated after his death, Alyosha allows his friend Rakitin to take him to see Grushenka. Although Rakitin and Grushenka hope to corrupt Alyosha, just the opposite happens, and a bond of sympathy and understanding springs up between Grushenka and Alyosha. Their friendship renews Alyosha's faith, and Alyosha helps Grushenka to begin her own spiritual redemption. That night, Alyosha has a dream in which Zosima tells him that he has done a good deed in helping Grushenka. This dream further strengthens Alyosha's love and resolve, and he goes outside to kiss the ground to show his passion for doing good on Earth.

Dmitri has spent two days unsuccessfully trying to raise the money to pay Katerina the 3,000 rubles he owes her. No one will lend him the money, and he has nothing to sell. At last he goes to Grushenka's house, and when she is not there, he is suddenly convinced that she has gone to be with Fyodor Pavlovich. He rushes to Fyodor Pavlovich's house, but finds that Grushenka is not there. While prowling on the grounds, Dmitri strikes Fyodor Pavlovich's old servant, Grigory, leaving him bloody and unconscious. Then he flees. He returns to Grushenka's house, and learns from her maid that Grushenka has gone to rejoin a lover who abandoned her several years ago. Dmitri now decides that his only course of action is to kill himself. But he decides to see Grushenka one last time before he does so.

A few minutes later, Dmitri strides into a shop, with his shirt bloody and a large wad of cash in his hand. He buys food and wine, and travels out to see Grushenka and her lover. When Grushenka sees the two men together, she realizes that she really loves Dmitri. Dmitri locks the other man in a closet, and Dmitri and Grushenka begin to plan their wedding. But the police suddenly burst in and arrest Dmitri. He is accused of the murder of his father, who has been found dead. Due to the large amount of evidence against Dmitri, including the money suddenly found in his possession, he will be made to stand trial. Dmitri says that the money was what he had left after spending half of the 3,000 rubles he stole from Katerina, but no one believes him. Dmitri is imprisoned.

Meanwhile, Alyosha befriends some of the local schoolboys. He meets a dying boy named Ilyusha, and arranges for the other boys to come visit him every day. Alyosha helps Ilyusha's family as the young boy nears death, and he is universally adored by all the schoolboys, who look to him for guidance.

Ivan talks to Smerdyakov about Fyodor Pavlovich's death, and Smerdyakov confesses to Ivan that he, and not Dmitri, committed the murder. But he says that Ivan is also implicated in the crime because the philosophical lessons Smerdyakov learned from Ivan, regarding the impossibility of evil in a world without a God, made Smerdyakov capable of committing murder. This statement causes Ivan to become consumed with guilt. After returning home, Ivan suffers a nervous breakdown in which he sees a devil that relentlessly taunts him. The apparition vanishes when Alyosha arrives with the news that Smerdyakov has hung himself.

At the trial, Dmitri's case seems to be going well until Ivan is called upon to testify. Ivan madly asserts that he himself is guilty of the murder, throwing the courtroom into confusion. To clear Ivan's name, Katerina leaps up and shows a letter she received from Dmitri in which he wrote that he was afraid he might one day murder his father. Even after the letter is read, most of the people in the courtroom are convinced of Dmitri's innocence. But the peasants on the jury find him guilty, and he is taken back to prison to await his exile in Siberia.

After the trial, Katerina takes Ivan to her house, where she plans to nurse him through his illness. She and Dmitri forgive one another, and she arranges for Dmitri to escape from prison and flee to America with Grushenka. Alyosha's friend Ilyusha dies, and Alyosha gives a speech to the schoolboys at his funeral. In plain language, he says that they must all remember the love they feel for one another and treasure their memories of one another. The schoolboys, moved, give Alyosha an enthusiastic cheer.

CHARACTER LIST

A NOTE ON THE NAMES

To English-speaking readers, the names of the characters in *The Brothers Karamazov* can be confusing. Characters are often referred to formally, with both their first and middle names: "Fyodor Pavlovich" or "Dmitri Fyodorovich." In these cases, the middle names are almost always based on the name of the character's father. As a result, the Karamazov brothers all have the middle name "Fyodorovich," meaning literally, "son of Fyodor." We learn very little about the father of Karamazov's first wife, Adelaida Ivanovna, but from her middle name, we know that his name was Ivan. Keeping this device in mind can be a helpful way to distinguish the characters early in the novel when a character's father also takes part in the story.

When characters are not referred to in the formal manner, they are often referred to by informal nicknames, which may seem to bear little resemblance to their real names: Alexei Karamazov is called "Alyosha" throughout the novel, and Dmitri Karamazov is frequently called "Mitka." Many characters have multiple nicknames. In the list that follows, each character's most common nicknames are given in parentheses after the character's full name. If the character is frequently called by one of many nicknames, the frequently used name is italicized.

Alexei Fyodorovich Karamazov (*Alyosha*, Alyoshka, Alyoshenka, Alyoshechka, Alxeichick, Lyosha, Lyoshenka) The protagonist, the third son of Fyodor Pavlovich Karamazov, and the younger brother of Dmitri and Ivan. Kind, gentle, loving, and wise, Alyosha is the opposite of his coarse and vulgar father. He possesses a natural, simple faith in God that translates into a genuine love for mankind. Around twenty years old at the start of the novel, Alyosha is affiliated with the monastery, where he is a student of the elder Zosima.

Dmitri Fyodorovich Karamazov (**Mitka,** Mitya, Mitenka, Mitri Fyodorovich) The oldest son of Fyodor Pavlovich Karamazov. Dmitri is passionate and intemperate, easily swept away by emotions and enthusiasms, as he demonstrates when he loses interest in his fiancée Katerina and falls madly in love with Grushenka. Cursed with a violent temper, Dmitri is plagued with the burden of sin and struggles throughout the novel to overcome his own flawed nature and to attain spiritual redemption.

Ivan Fyodorovich Karamazov (Vanya, Vanka, Vanechka) The second son of Fyodor Pavlovich Karamazov, and the middle brother between Dmitri and Alyosha. A brilliant student, Ivan has an acutely logical mind and demands a rational explanation for everything that happens in the universe. As a result of his inability to reconcile the idea of unjust suffering with the idea of a loving God, Ivan is plagued by religious doubt, and he oscillates between outright atheism and belief in a malevolent God. His forceful arguments about God's cruelty toward mankind are compelling, but after they lead to the murder of his father, they drive him into madness.

Fyodor Pavlovich Karamazov The wealthy patriarch of the Karamazov dynasty, the father of Alyosha, Dmitri, and Ivan, and almost certainly the father of Smerdyakov. Coarse, vulgar, greedy, and lustful, Fyodor Pavlovich lives a life devoted exclusively to the satisfaction of his senses, with no thought for those whom he betrays or hurts. Completely lacking in dignity despite his wealth, Fyodor Pavlovich is loathed by almost everyone who knows him. He has no affection for his children, and even forgets which of them belongs to which mother. His only goal in life is to have money and seduce young women such as Grushenka, whom he lusts after for much of the novel. Fyodor Pavlovich is eventually murdered by Smerdyakov.

Agrafena Alexandrovna Svetlov (**Grushenka,** Grusha, Grushka) A beautiful young woman who is brought to the town by Samsonov after a lover betrays her. Proud, fiery, and headstrong, Grushenka is an almost universal object of desire among the men in the town and is the source of much of the antagonism between Fyodor Pavlovich and Dmitri. She is reputed to be sexually promiscuous, but in reality, she is much too proud to give herself to lovers. She devotes herself instead to increasing her wealth by making shrewd investments, but after she meets Alyosha, a hidden vein of gentleness and love begins to emerge in her character.

Pavel Fyodorovich Smerdyakov The son of Lizaveta and Fyodor Pavlovich Karamazov, Smerdyakov is raised by Grigory and his wife Marfa and is made to work in Fyodor Pavlovich's house as a servant. Cursed with epilepsy, Smerdyakov also has a mean temperament, sometimes exhibiting outright malice and sometimes hiding behind a mask of groveling servitude. He is particularly interested in discussing philosophy with Ivan, whose advocacy of an antireligious amorality paves the way for Smerdyakov to murder Fyodor Pavlovich.

Zosima The wise elder at the monastery who acts as Alyosha's mentor and teacher before his death in Book VI. Extremely intelligent and filled with an ardent and sincere religious faith, Zosima preaches a message of actively loving mankind, forgiving the sins of others, and cherishing God's creation. The clarity of Zosima's faith gives him extraordinary insight into the minds of the people he meets.

Katerina Ivanovna Verkhovtsev (**Katya,** Katka, Katenka) Dmitri's fiancée, whom he abandons after falling in love with Grushenka. The proud and sensitive daughter of a military captain, Katerina anguishes over her ill treatment by Dmitri, which leads her to adopt an attitude of martyrdom toward those around her. She insists on humiliating herself with an unfailing loyalty to the people who hurt her, and though she loves Ivan, she is unable to act on her love until the end of the novel.

Katerina Ospovna Khokhlakov (**Madame Khokhlakov**) A wealthy gentlewoman in the town, an acquaintance of the Karamazovs and a friend of Katerina. A relatively harmless presence, she is somewhat shallow and self-centered, and tends to obsess over the misbehaviors of her daughter Lise.

Liza Khokhlakov (**Lise**) Madame Khokhlakov's daughter, a mischievous and capricious young girl who is briefly engaged to Alyosha. At least as shallow and self-centered as her mother, Lise has a hard time taking things seriously and finally lapses into a kind of self-destructive despair, in which she pathetically crushes her fingernail in a door in an attempt to punish herself for wickedness.

Mikhail Osipovich Rakitin A young seminary student whom Alyosha considers a friend, but who secretly despises him. Cynical and sarcastic, Rakitin is too sophisticated to have real religious faith, so he satisfies himself with adopting various fashionable philosophical theories. He quotes Nietzsche and claims to be a socialist. Deeply threatened by Alyosha's apparently genuine moral purity, Rakitin secretly longs to see Alyosha become corrupted. As a result, he tries very hard to introduce Alyosha to Grushenka, whom he believes will shake Alyosha's faith.

Pyotr Alexandrovich Miusov A wealthy landowner, the cousin of Fyodor Pavlovich Karamazov's first wife, and briefly the guardian of the young Dmitri. Considering himself a political intellectual, Miusov utterly despises Fyodor Pavlovich.

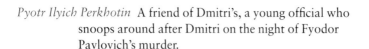

Pyotr Ilyich Perkhotin A friend of Dmitri's, a young official who snoops around after Dmitri on the night of Fyodor Pavlovich's murder.

Kuzma Kuzmich Samsonov The old merchant who brings Grushenka to the town after her former lover betrays her.

Stinking Lizaveta A young retarded girl who lives as the village idiot. She dies giving birth to Smerdyakov, leading most people to suspect that Fyodor Pavlovich Karamazov either seduced or raped her.

Fetyukovich A famous defense attorney from Moscow who represents Dmitri at the trial.

Ippolit Kirrillovich The prosecuting attorney at Dmitri's trial.

Father Ferapont A severe and ascetic monk who hates Zosima.

Nikolai Ivanov Krasotkin (*Kolya*) A bold, intelligent young boy who befriends Alyosha after Ilyusha becomes ill.

Ilyusha Snegiryov (Ilyushechka, Ilyushka) The son of a military captain, who once saw his father beaten up by Dmitri. Proud and unwilling to be cowed by the larger boys who pick on him, Ilyusha befriends Alyosha, but becomes ill and dies toward the end of the novel.

Grigory Kutuzov Vasilievich Fyodor Pavlovich Karamazov's servant, who, along with his wife Marfa, raises Smerdyakov from birth.

CHARACTER LIST

ANALYSIS OF MAJOR CHARACTERS

ALYOSHA

The narrator describes Alyosha as the "hero" of *The Brothers Kara-mazov* and claims that the book is Alyosha's "biography." A young, handsome man of about twenty, Alyosha is remarkable for his extraordinarily mature religious faith, his selflessness, and his innate love of humankind. Alyosha is naturally good: his love of his fellow human beings is simply a part of his personality, and he rarely has to struggle against temptation or doubt. He spends his energy doing good deeds for his fellow men and trying as honestly as he can to help them become happier and more fulfilled. Alyosha is not judgmental and has an uncanny ability to understand the psychology of others. Despite his infallible goodness and his natural advantages, Alyosha has a gentle, easygoing personality that causes almost everyone who knows him to love him.

At the same time, Alyosha is not naïve or innocent. He understands human evil and the burden of sin, but he practices universal forgiveness. Alyosha's religious faith is the cornerstone of his character. His faith in a loving God, strengthened by his close relationship with the monastic elder Zosima, reinforces his love of mankind and his immense capability to do good. Even when Alyosha experiences doubt, his doubt is always resolved by his commitment to do good. At the end of the novel, Alyosha has become the mature embodiment of Zosima's teachings, and he even helps to guarantee Zosima's legacy by spreading his teachings among the young schoolboys of the town, who adore him.

Alyosha is an unusual main character because he does not initiate much of the main action of the novel. Instead, he tends to react calmly to whatever the other characters are driven by passion. But *The Brothers Karamazov* is a novel that analyzes various ways of life—the coarse sensualism of Fyodor Pavlovich and the cold skepticism of Ivan both come under scrutiny—and questions each of them sharply. Alyosha's way of life seems superior to that of the other characters. He is the moral center of the novel because he represents the model of attitude and behavior that Dostoevsky considers the right one, the one most conducive to human happiness and peace instead of the trauma and conflict that afflict most of the novel's other major characters.

IVAN

No character in *The Brothers Karamazov* is afflicted with more trauma or inner conflict than Ivan. Ivan is a brilliant student with an incisively analytical mind, and his intelligence is directly to blame for his descent into despair. Unable to reconcile the horror of unjust human suffering—particularly the suffering of children—with the idea of a loving God, Ivan is consumed with doubt and argues that even if God does exist, he is malicious and hostile, and loves to torture mankind. Ivan believes that human concepts of morality are dependent on the idea that the soul is immortal, meaning that people only worry about "right" and "wrong" behavior because they want to experience pleasure rather than pain in the afterlife. Because of his feelings about God, Ivan himself is unable to believe in the immortality of the soul, and thus he argues that good and evil are fraudulent categories, and that people may do whatever they wish without regard for morality. But Ivan only starts thinking about these concepts in the first place because he loves humanity—it is his concern for human suffering that initially leads him to reject God. His logical disbelief in morality is terribly painful for him because it would make a way of life such as Fyodor Pavlovich's, which Ivan detests, an acceptable mode of human behavior. Dignified and coldly moral, Ivan wants to be able to accept an idea of goodness that would exalt mankind and reject Fyodor Pavlovich's brutishness, but, trapped in his own logic, he is unable to do so. He is so beset with doubt, and so defensively determined to keep the rest of humanity at a distance, that he is unable to act on his love for Katerina, and seems to scorn the very thought of pursuing happiness for himself.

After Smerdyakov murders Fyodor Pavlovich, Ivan's crisis of faith becomes more traumatic still. Convinced by Smerdyakov that Ivan's philosophy made it possible for Smerdyakov to kill Fyodor Pavlovich, Ivan is forced to confront two very difficult notions: first, that he is responsible for another human being, and second, that his beliefs have paved the way for murder. Ivan's subsequent collapse into hallucination and madness represents the novel's final rejection of his skeptical way of life. When the novel ends, Ivan is feverish and

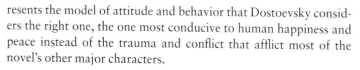

unconscious, having been taken home by Katerina to recuperate, and his future is uncertain. It may be that, with Katerina's love, he will find a way to accept Alyosha's faith or come to terms intellectually with morality and his own responsibility for others. Or it may be that he will never resolve his crisis—he may become permanently insane. But the extremely optimistic note on which the novel ends suggests that he will find some form of redemption.

Dmitri

Dmitri is the most turbulent of the three brothers. Passionate, headstrong, and reckless, he combines Alyosha's good heart with Fyodor Pavlovich's heedless sensuality. Dmitri has lived a life torn between sin and redemption. Unlike Alyosha, Dmitri is dominated by his passions, but unlike Fyodor Pavlovich, he feels genuine remorse for the sins he has committed and gradually comes to hope that his soul can be redeemed through suffering. Because Dmitri is the character most poised between animalism and spiritual redemption, he often represents the plight of humanity itself in the novel. When he is arrested for the murder of Fyodor Pavlovich, the question of his guilt or innocence becomes a crucial question about human nature—whether it is founded on good or evil. Dmitri is not only innocent of the crime, he undergoes an ardent spiritual conversion in prison and emerges from his trial a stronger, better person, prepared to live a life of goodness and to do penance for his sins. Through Dmitri's redemption and Ivan's breakdown, Dostoevsky thus concludes the novel by rejecting doubt and skepticism in favor of faith and love. Dmitri's redemption represents the novel's optimistic conclusion about the nature of mankind.

THEMES, MOTIFS & SYMBOLS

THEMES

Themes are the fundamental and often universal ideas explored in a literary work.

THE CONFLICT BETWEEN FAITH AND DOUBT

The central philosophical conflict of *The Brothers Karamazov* is the conflict between religious faith and doubt. The main characters illustrate the different kinds of behavior that these two positions generate. Faith in the novel refers to the positive, assenting belief in God practiced by Zosima and Alyosha, which lends itself to an active love of mankind, kindness, forgiveness, and a devotion to goodness. Doubt refers to the kind of logical skepticism that Ivan Karamazov practices, which, in pursuing the truth through the logical examination of evidence, lends itself to the rejection of God, the rejection of conventional notions of morality, a coldness toward mankind, and a crippling inner despair. Dostoevsky does not present these positions neutrally. He actively takes the side of faith, and illustrates through innumerable examples how a life of faith is happier than a life of doubt. Doubt, as we see in Smerdyakov's murder of Fyodor Pavlovich and in Ivan's breakdown, leads only to chaos and unhappiness. But the novel nevertheless examines the psychology of doubt with great objectivity and rigor. Through the character of Ivan, in chapters such as "The Grand Inquisitor," Dostoevsky presents an incisive case against religion, the Church, and God, suggesting that the choice to embrace religious faith can only be made at great philosophical risk, and for reasons that defy a fully logical explanation.

THE BURDEN OF FREE WILL

The novel argues forcefully that people have free will, whether they wish to or not. That is, every individual is free to choose whether to believe or disbelieve in God, whether to accept or reject morality, and whether to pursue good or evil. The condition of free will may seem to be a blessing, guaranteeing the spiritual independence of each individual and ensuring that no outside force can control the individual's choices with regard to faith. But throughout *The Brothers Karamazov*, Dostoevsky portrays free will as a curse, one that particularly plagues those characters who have chosen to doubt God's existence. Free will can be seen as a curse because it places a crippling burden on humanity to voluntarily reject the securities, comforts, and protections of the world in favor of the uncertainties and hardships of religious belief. Most people are too weak to make this choice, Ivan argues, and most people are doomed to unhappy lives that end in eternal damnation. The Grand Inquisitor story in Book V explores Christ's biblical rejection of the temptations offered to him by Satan and concludes that Christ was wrong to have rejected them, since his rejection won free will for humanity, but took away security. Nevertheless, the condition of free will is finally shown to be a necessary component of the simple and satisfying faith practiced by Alyosha and Zosima, and the novel's optimistic conclusion suggests that perhaps people are not as weak as Ivan believes them to be.

THE PERVASIVENESS OF MORAL RESPONSIBILITY

One of the central lessons of the novel is that people should not judge one another, should forgive one another's sins, and should pray for the redemption of criminals rather than their punishment. Zosima explains that this loving forgiveness is necessary because the chain of human causation is so interwoven that everyone bears some responsibility for the sins of everyone else. That is, one person's actions have so many complicated effects on the actions of so many other people that it is impossible to trace all the consequences of any single action. Everything we do is influenced by innumerable actions of those around us, and as a result, no one can be held singly responsible for a crime or for a sin. This idea of shared responsibility is abhorrent to characters in the novel who doubt God and Christianity, especially Ivan, who repeatedly insists that he is not responsible for the actions of anyone but himself. Ivan's arguments counter a belief in mutual responsibility, since he believes that without God or an afterlife, there is no moral law. In a world in which the absence of God makes moral distinctions meaningless, people are logically justified in simply acting out their desires. Additionally, Ivan's deep distrust of human nature makes him inclined to keep the rest of humanity at a chilly distance, and the idea that the things he does affect other people makes him emotionally uncomfortable. When Smerdyakov explains to Ivan how Ivan's amoral philosophical beliefs have made it possible for Smerdyakov to kill Fyodor Pavlovich, Ivan is suddenly forced to accept the harshest consequences of his relentless skepticism: not only has his doubt paved the way for murder, but he has no choice but to admit his own complicity in the execution of that murder. Ivan suddenly understands the nature of moral responsibility as it has been explained by Zosima, and the sudden comprehension is so overwhelming that it leads to a nervous breakdown—Dostoevsky's final depiction of the consequences of doubt.

MOTIFS

Motifs are recurring structures, contrasts, or literary devices that can help to develop and inform the text's major themes.

CRIME AND JUSTICE

In the context of the novel's larger exploration of sin, redemption, and justice, a major motif in the novel is the idea of crime and criminal justice. The crimes portrayed in the novel are also sins, or crimes against God, and the novel presents them in such a way as to suggest that human beings are not capable of passing judgment on one another. The only true judge, as we see in the aftermath of Dmitri's wrongful conviction, is the conscience. Images of criminal justice in the novel occur most prominently in the debate between Ivan and the monks about ecclesiastical courts, in the story of the Grand Inquisitor, and in Dmitri's arrest, imprisonment, and trial.

REDEMPTION THROUGH SUFFERING

A central part of Dostoevsky's exploration of spiritual redemption is the idea that self-knowledge is necessary for a person to be redeemed. As Zosima explains in Book I, only when a man knows himself and faces himself honestly can he come to love others and love God. The principal way to arrive at that self-knowledge is through suffering. Suffering can occur either through the grief and guilt of sin, or, as in the case of Grushenka and Ivan, through the agony of illnesses that are metaphors for spiritual conditions. Apart from the sufferings of Grushenka and Ivan, the other major embodiment of this motif in the novel is Dmitri, who suffers through the misery of realizing his own evil before he can embrace his goodness. When Lise willfully slams her fingers in the door, she provides another, bitterly ironic instance of the motif. Lise wants to punish herself for being wicked, but her idea of suffering is so shallow, vain, and ridiculous that it is not really a serious attempt at redemption.

THE PROFOUND GESTURE

Although *The Brothers Karamazov* is fundamentally an exploration of religious faith, the novel supports the idea that the choice to believe in God cannot be fully explained in rational terms. Profound, inexplicable gestures often take the place of argumentative dialogue. These gestures defy explanation, but convey a poetic sense of the qualities that make faith necessary and satisfying for the human soul. Examples of these profound, enigmatic gestures include Zosima kneeling before Dmitri in Book I, Christ kissing the Grand Inquisitor in Book V, Alyosha kissing Ivan in the same book, Zosima embracing the Earth just before he dies in Book VI, and Alyosha kissing the ground after his dream in Book VII. Each of these gestures can only be partially explained. Zosima, for example, kneels before Dmitri to acknowledge the suffering Dmitri will face. But none of these gestures can be fully explained, and their ambiguity is a way of challenging the rational paradigm that Ivan embraces.

SYMBOLS

Symbols are objects, characters, figures, or colors used to represent abstract ideas or concepts.

CHARACTERS AS SYMBOLS

Because *The Brothers Karamazov* is both a realistic novel and a philosophical novel, Dostoevsky's characterizations tend to yield fully drawn, believable individuals who also represent certain qualities and ideas bearing on the larger philosophical argument. The drama acted out between the characters becomes the drama of the larger ideas in conflict with one another. Most of the important symbols in the novel, then, are characters. Almost every major character in the novel embodies a concept: Alyosha represents faith, Ivan represents doubt, and Fyodor Pavlovich represents selfishness and physical appetite. Some characters have more specific designations. Smerdyakov, for instance, works primarily as a living symbol of Fyodor Pavlovich's wickedness.

ZOSIMA'S CORPSE

The monks, including Alyosha, all expect Zosima's death to be followed by a great miracle that will commemorate his extraordinary wisdom and virtue in life. They even expect that he will prove to be a saint. In monastic lore, one of the ways in which a saint can be detected after death is that his corpse, rather than emitting the stench of decay, is instead suffused with a pleasant smell. After Zosima's death, however, no miracle occurs. Moreover, Zosima's corpse begins to stink very quickly, exuding a particularly strong and putrid odor, which is taken by his enemies in the monastery as proof of his inner corruption. For Alyosha, who craves a miracle, the indignity visited upon Zosima's corpse exemplifies the lack of validation with which the world often rewards religious faith. The fate of Zosima's corpse suggests that faith is not justified by miracles. Rather, the person who chooses faith must do so in defiance of the many reasons to doubt.

SYMBOLS

Summary & Analysis

Author's Note & Book I: A Nice Little Family, Chapters 1–5

> *Above all, do not lie to yourself. A man who lies to himself and listens to his own lie comes to a point where he does not discern any truth either in himself or anywhere around him. . . .*
>
> *(See* Quotations, *p. 75)*

Summary — From the Author

In a short introduction, the author—writing in the somewhat comical and haphazard style employed by the narrator throughout the novel—poses the question of why anyone should read his story, which he describes as the "biography" of Alyosha. He concludes that the story describes an odd man who nevertheless captures something essential about his time. The author apologizes for the fragmentary nature of his story, but says that he hopes readers will read it to the end. He also apologizes for wasting his readers' time with a superfluous author's note.

Summary — Chapter 1: Fyodor Pavlovich Karamazov

Alexei Fyodorovich Karamazov, usually called Alyosha, is the third son of a brutish landowner named Fyodor Pavlovich Karamazov, who is still famous for his dark and violent death. The narrator tells the story of Fyodor Pavlovich's life. As a young man, he is known as a loutish buffoon. He owns a very small amount of land and earns a reputation for sponging off other people. Nevertheless, he somehow manages to marry a rich, beautiful, intelligent girl named Adelaida Ivanovna Miusova, who convinces herself that eloping with a bold and sarcastic man like Fyodor Pavlovich is a romantic thing to do. After they are married, Adelaida Ivanovna realizes that she feels nothing but contempt for Fyodor Pavlovich, and when their son, Dmitri, is three, she runs away with a poor seminary student, leaving Fyodor Pavlovich with the boy. Fyodor Pavlovich begins traveling around the province, tearfully complaining about his wife's desertion. In Adelaida Ivanovna's absence, however, Fyodor Pavlovich turns his house into a harem and spends much of his time indulging in drunken orgies financed by the fortune he has filched from Adelaida Ivanovna. When Fyodor Pavlovich hears that Adelaida Ivanovna has died from starvation or disease in a Petersburg garret, he runs down the street drunkenly celebrating his freedom. There is another version of this story, however, which says that Fyodor Pavlovich instead weeps like a child. The narrator says both versions of the story may be true: Fyodor Pavlovich may have simultaneously rejoiced and mourned his wife's death, for even wicked people like Fyodor Pavlovich are generally more naïve and simple than one is inclined to suspect.

SUMMARY—CHAPTER 2: THE FIRST SON SENT PACKING
As soon as Adelaida Ivanovna flees from her marriage to Fyodor Pavlovich, Fyodor Pavlovich forgets all about his three-year-old son. For a year, a servant raises the neglected Dmitri. Dmitri is then passed around among a number of his mother's relatives, including her cousin Pyotr Alexandrovich Miusov. These relatives lead Dmitri to believe that he has inherited some his mother's money and property, which is now in the care of his father. After a wild young adulthood and a stint in the army, Dmitri visits his father to learn the details of his inheritance. Fyodor Pavlovich evades Dmitri's questions and gives him a small sum of money to quiet him. After Dmitri leaves, his father successfully manipulates him by sending him other small payments, which lead Dmitri to believe that he has a sizable inheritance. But when Dmitri next visits his father, Fyodor Pavlovich tells him that he has paid out all the money from his mother's inheritance, and that Dmitri might even owe a small sum to his father. Dmitri, stunned, quickly concludes that his father is attempting to cheat him, and he remains in the town to fight what he believes is his father's unwillingness to hand over the fortune that is rightfully Dmitri's.

SUMMARY—CHAPTER 3: SECOND MARRIAGE, SECOND CHILDREN
Fyodor Pavlovich remarries soon after getting rid of four-year-old Dmitri. He stays married for about eight years. His wife, Sofia Ivanovna, is a sixteen-year-old orphan from another province, where Fyodor Pavlovich has traveled on a business trip. Despite his drunken and debauched lifestyle, Fyodor Pavlovich has handled his investments shrewdly, and his fortune continues to grow. Fyodor Pavlovich convinces Sofia to elope with him against the wishes of her guardian, and Fyodor Pavlovich treats her deplorably, openly

holding orgies with other women in the house, right under her nose. As a result of Fyodor Pavlovich's ill treatment, Sofia becomes nervous and hysterical, until her husband begins calling her "the shrieker." Despite her instability, Sofia gives birth to two sons, Ivan and Alexei, who is nicknamed Alyosha. When Alyosha is four, Sofia dies, and the two boys fall into the care of the same servant who briefly had charge of Dmitri. Their mother's former guardian, a general's widow, then takes them in. The widow soon dies, but leaves funds for the education of Alyosha and Ivan. As the boys grow older, in the care of their benefactress's heir, Ivan becomes a brilliant student, gaining notoriety in literary circles for an article he writes about ecclesiastical courts. Eventually Ivan moves back to his father's town to live with his father, despite having been ashamed of him all his life. This bizarre circumstance is partially arranged by Dmitri, who, after being told about his ruined inheritance, has requested that his brother join him and their father, hoping that Ivan might help to mediate their dispute.

Summary — Chapter 4: The Third Son, Alyosha

Alyosha is twenty years old when Dmitri moves to their father's home. Alyosha has lived in the monastery in his father's town for about a year before his brothers' arrival. He is religious—not in a mystical or superstitious way, but simply out of a generous and innate love of humankind. Alyosha even seems to love his father and is never critical of him or unkind to him. Everyone loves Alyosha, for despite his tendency to remain detached from others, he exudes a kind of blissful serenity. He has been extremely popular as a student despite his passive nature and his innocence—the only thing the other students ever tease him about is the acute embarrassment he feels whenever the topics of women or sex arise. After Alyosha moves back to his father's town, he quickly grows close to Fyodor Pavlovich, who uncharacteristically donates a great deal of money to the monastery after Alyosha visits his mother's grave. Fyodor Pavlovich becomes very sentimental when Alyosha tells him that he intends to enter the monastery and study under the elder Zosima.

Summary — Chapter 5: Elders

Alyosha is greatly moved by the arrival of his brothers. He quickly becomes close to Dmitri, but he feels that Ivan's cold intellectualism keeps him distant from others. Alyosha senses that Ivan is struggling toward an inner goal that makes him indifferent to the outside world. Dmitri and Ivan are as unlike as two people can be, but Alyosha notices that Dmitri speaks of Ivan with warmth and admiration.

Dmitri has become embroiled with their father in a conflict over the inheritance, and it is finally arranged that the two parties will have a discussion in Zosima's cell, where the presence of the influential monk might help them resolve their differences. The prospect of this meeting makes Alyosha nervous—he knows that his father would only agree to such a thing sarcastically, and that Ivan himself is an atheist. He worries that his family's behavior will offend Zosima, whom he esteems very highly and who acts as his spiritual leader within the monastery.

ANALYSIS—AUTHOR'S NOTE AND BOOK I: A NICE LITTLE FAMILY, CHAPTERS 1–5

Book I provides a history of the major characters and their relationships, so the narrator can jump right into the main story in Book II without stopping to explain things as he goes. The narrator presents all of the incidents described in these chapters as though they take place before the real beginning of his story, describing the events as information that is generally well-known, repeated only for the convenience of a reader who somehow may not have heard it before. The narrator, as a result, is a strong presence in these chapters. The narrator signals that the story he tells is widely known by interjecting phrases such as "only later did we learn" and "well known in his own day."

The Brothers Karamazov is a cross between a realistic novel and a philosophical novel. The characters have extremely complicated and intricate psychologies, and yet they also each represent certain ideas and concepts. This combination of realism and philosophical symbolism is evident in these chapters, as each meticulously drawn character comes to embody a more abstract set of concepts and beliefs. Fyodor Pavlovich Karamazov, the father, with his orgies and his abhorrent treatment of his wives and children, embodies amoral, obnoxious Epicureanism—that is, a commitment to seeking pleasure rather than living responsibly or virtuously. Ivan Karamazov's brilliant mind and burgeoning literary reputation embody the struggle to reconcile intellect with religious belief. Dmitri Karamazov's violent hatred of his father and uncritical love of his brothers stand in opposition to Ivan's critical faculties. Dmitri's character illustrates the effects of action based on emotion rather than on intellect. Finally, Alyosha, whom Dostoevsky describes as the hero of the novel, is nearly the opposite of Fyodor Pavlovich. His love of mankind shows that he is innocent, pious, and virtuous without being mystical or fanatical.

Each character in Dostoevsky's quartet of personalities works as a foil, or contrast, for each of the others. Because the novel's philosophical themes are immediately connected to the personalities of its characters, the conflicts and contrasts between the main characters come to symbolize some of the most fundamental problems of human existence. The difference between Ivan and Alyosha, for instance, represents the conflict between faith and doubt. Though none of these philosophical issues are given extensive treatment in this section, each of them, along with many others, is expanded and developed as the novel progresses. In the end, the story of the Karamazov brothers enacts a part of the drama of ideas on which civilization itself is based.

There are several religious concepts in these chapters that may be unfamiliar to modern readers who are not members of the Russian Orthodox church, to which the Karamazovs belong. First, the article for which Ivan has gained notoriety before the story begins deals with the question of ecclesiastical courts. These are simply courts of law, which decide cases based not on the political laws that govern nations, but on religious law and the strictures of the church. Ecclesiastical courts in Russia at the time of the novel do not have the power to try or punish criminals. Ivan's article argues that ecclesiastical courts should be given authority over criminal prosecution and punishment because if criminals knew they were defying God when they committed their crimes, many of them would choose to obey the law. Given Ivan's reputation for religious doubt, many of the people who know him suspect that he does not entirely believe his own argument. Ivan's argument is motivated not by a desire to punish, but, paradoxically, by compassion for mankind. He believes that without religious authority, people will descend into lawlessness and chaos. At the same time, because he does not believe in the church, Ivan rejects the notion of a binding morality. His article is sincere in that he believes his recommendations would improve the human condition, but insincere in that he does not believe in the ideas and institutions under which his recommendations would be carried out. The article, and the larger debate about ecclesiastical courts, thus serves to offer a preliminary insight into the nature of Ivan's anguished mind: he is so committed to intellectual logic that he is led to advocate ideas he does not believe in his heart.

BOOK II: AN INAPPROPRIATE GATHERING, CHAPTERS 1–4

SUMMARY—CHAPTER 1: THEY ARRIVE AT THE MONASTERY

On a warm, clear day at the end of August, Fyodor Pavlovich and Ivan Karamazov arrive at the monastery for the meeting with Zosima. Pyotr Alexandrovich Miusov, the cousin of Fyodor Pavlovich's first wife who briefly adopted the young Dmitri, is with them, as is Kalganov, a young relative of Miusov's who is living with him while preparing to enter a university. None of the men knows much about religion. Miusov, an atheist, has not been in a church for three decades. The men look around the monastery curiously. Miusov detests Fyodor Pavlovich, who intentionally torments Miusov by mocking the monastery and pretending not to understand why Miusov, as an irreligious man, would care what the monks think of him. Miusov angrily chastises himself for letting Fyodor Pavlovich bother him, but Fyodor Pavlovich's crudeness and vulgarity are so exasperating to Miusov that he cannot control his irritation.

Dmitri has not yet arrived, and the men are shown to Zosima's cell to wait. The little monk who escorts them tells them that they are all invited to lunch with the Father Superior of the monastery after their meeting.

SUMMARY—CHAPTER 2: THE OLD BUFFOON

The men enter Zosima's room just as Zosima himself arrives there, accompanied by Alyosha and a small group of monks. The monks kiss Zosima's hand in deference and ask for his blessing, but the other men decline to do so and merely bow to him somewhat stiffly. Alyosha is embarrassed by this awkward display of disrespect, but Zosima gives no sign of being troubled.

Fyodor Pavlovich apologizes melodramatically for Dmitri's lateness and fills the awkward silence in the room with his chatter. Under the pretense of being apologetic for his uncontrollably buffoonish behavior, Fyodor Pavlovich indulges in a series of increasingly sacrilegious witticisms and stories, well aware that in doing so, he is embarrassing and irritating the other men, especially Miusov, whom he relentlessly teases. Alyosha is mortified by his father's behavior, but Zosima does not seem to mind it. When Fyodor begins to play the supplicant and asks Zosima for spiritual advice, Alyosha is even more humiliated. But Zosima merely tells him that, if he wants to attain eternal life, he must stop telling lies, especially to himself. Surprisingly, Zosima attributes Fyodor Pavlovich's clownish behavior to the fact that Fyodor Pavlovich is embarrassed and ashamed of himself, and Zosima earnestly tries to make him more comfortable.

SUMMARY — CHAPTER 3: WOMEN OF FAITH

While the group waits for Dmitri, Zosima goes outside to meet with a crowd of women who have come to ask for his spiritual advice and blessings. Most of these women have endured great hardships and have come to Zosima for guidance. Zosima soothes a hysterical woman by covering her with his stole, then hears the story of a woman who has traveled two hundred miles to see him. After her three-year-old son died, she was overwhelmed with grief and left her husband. He tells her to weep for her son, but to remember with each tear that he is now an angel with God. He also tells her to return to her husband, so that her son's spirit will be able to stay near his parents. A woman whose son has traveled to Siberia with the army asks if it would be acceptable to publish his name among the dead in the church in order to shame him into writing her. Zosima tells her that to do so would be a great sin. A haggard woman tells Zosima about her husband, who beat her. She then whispers something in Zosima's ear, implying that she murdered her husband. Zosima tells her that God forgives all sins, and as long as she lives in perpetual repentance and loves God, her sin will be forgiven too. Another woman gives Zosima some money to give to a woman poorer than herself, and Zosima blesses her and her baby daughter.

SUMMARY — CHAPTER 4: A LADY OF LITTLE FAITH

Zosima then speaks to Madame Khokhlakov, a wealthy landowner who has met him before, and her daughter Lise, a girl with a mischievous look on her face. Madame Khokhlakov tells Zosima that his prayers have healed her daughter, who has been ill and unable to walk, but Zosima suspects that Lise's recovery is incomplete. Madame Khokhlakov says that she is beset with religious doubt—she not only has trouble believing in the immortality of the soul, she finds it impossible to perform charitable works without expecting praise and admiration in return. Zosima tells her not to worry, but to practice active, committed love for mankind, and God will forgive her flaws simply by virtue of the fact that she is aware of them. In the meantime, Lise teases the self-conscious Alyosha: Lise says that Alyosha was her childhood friend, but since he came to the monastery he never visits her anymore. Zosima warmly promises her that Alyosha will visit her soon.

ANALYSIS — BOOK II: AN INAPPROPRIATE GATHERING, CHAPTERS 1–4

Through the character of Zosima, Dostoevsky establishes a relationship between love and truth. As displayed in these chapters, the two qualities Zosima values above all others are love and honesty, particularly honesty with oneself. He connects these two ideas intimately: he tells both Fyodor Pavlovich and Madame Khokhlakov that they must be honest with themselves because a dishonest person loses the ability to distinguish truth from falsehood, and thus loses the ability to respect and love other people. In Zosima's view, the ability to love is based on the ability to recognize truth. He explains that if a person cannot believe in himself, he will quickly become suspicious of everyone around him, assuming that the world is full of lies. Because he cannot believe in his own perceptions, he will become unable to tell lies from truth, and because he is corrupted by his own dishonesty, he will suspect that everything is a lie. By becoming suspicious, he loses his respect for others and thus his ability to love them. This mode of reasoning represents a philosophy of doubt that opposes Alyosha's loving faith. The process described by Zosima here is an incredibly incisive description of Fyodor Pavlovich's personality and the road he has taken to arrive at it, but to a greater or lesser extent, it becomes relevant to nearly every character in the novel, including Ivan and Dmitri.

Ivan's speculation—if the soul is not immortal, then there is no morality at all, and people might as well live simply to satisfy their own selfish appetites—links the personality differences between the major characters to broad questions of philosophy and religious faith. Ivan's troubling hypothesis prompts us to consider the difference between Alyosha's selfless goodness and Fyodor Pavlovich's selfish evil. Zosima is thus a central character in the early part of the novel, even though his role in the larger narrative is comparatively small, because he draws the connections between faith and goodness for us, helping us to understand the main characters. He is the first character in the novel to articulate some of Dostoevsky's great themes. He is also important because of the role he plays in the mind of Alyosha, who venerates him absolutely. A great part of Alyosha's moral feeling—his kindness, his desire to help others, his modesty—has been influenced by Zosima, and through Alyosha, Zosima's example influences some of the most important actions in the novel.

Zosima's goodness causes us to see the flaws in the other characters. All of the other characters are troubled by some irritation or concern, some earthly flaw that makes them seem fallible and even petty in comparison to the saintly Zosima. Even Alyosha, who is relatively saintly himself, is made mortal in these chapters by his embarrassment over his family's behavior in front of Zosima, and later by his awkwardness around Lise. Miusov's flaw is his hatred of Fyodor Pavlovich, which fills him with an uncontrollable anger nearly every time Fyodor Pavlovich speaks. For his part, Fyodor Pavlovich is almost entirely fallible and flawed—he is obnoxious, disrespectful, vulgar, and dishonest, and he delights in intentionally irritating the other characters with his brutish humor and his buffoonery. The only person who is not made uncomfortable by Fyodor Pavlovich's brazen behavior is Zosima, which illustrates Zosima's own high level of spirituality. Only Zosima possesses the inner serenity and the unshakable love of mankind necessary to overlook Fyodor Pavlovich's ugly personality and tolerate his boorish behavior. Fyodor Pavlovich's children, as represented by Alyosha in this section, find him much harder to take.

BOOK II: AN INAPPROPRIATE GATHERING, CHAPTERS 5–8

SUMMARY—CHAPTER 5: SO BE IT! SO BE IT!

Alyosha follows Zosima back to his cell, where Ivan and the monks are debating Ivan's article about ecclesiastical courts. Miusov, who considers himself a political intellectual, continually tries to join the argument, but the other men, caught up in their own discussion, generally ignore him. Miusov, already aggravated by Fyodor Pavlovich's taunting, becomes almost unbearably irritated.

Ivan explains that he does not believe in the separation of the church and state. He believes that the church should subsume the state, so that religious authorities administer laws, and ecclesiastical courts handle the judicial process. Miusov tries to interject that this situation would be "sheer Ultramontanism," meaning that Ivan's proposal would create a situation in which the pope would have absolute power. The word Ultramontanism refers to the fact that Rome, the seat of the papacy of the Catholic Church, is literally "beyond the mountains" from Russia and the Orthodox Church. The other men ignore Miusov. Ivan insists that if the only courts were ecclesiastical courts, the very notion of crime would slowly change. People would be much less likely to commit crimes in the first place, he argues, because they would know that in doing so, they would be acting not merely against a government or a state, but against God.

Zosima, to the surprise of some of the others in the room, agrees with Ivan's analysis. He argues, however, that the only real power capable of punishing crime is conscience. He says that because the church knows that each individual's moral sense is the real authority, the church chooses not to become involved in the state's administration of justice. The men become so embroiled in their debate that they forget about Dmitri's lateness, and when he suddenly bursts in through the door, they are slightly surprised to see him.

SUMMARY—CHAPTER 6: WHY IS SUCH A MAN ALIVE!
Dmitri asks for Zosima's blessing and says that he is late because his father's messenger gave him the wrong time. Not wishing to interrupt the debate, Dmitri finds a chair and sits quietly. Ivan goes on to say that, in his view, the entire notion of morality depends on the idea of the immortality of the soul. If people did not believe in an afterlife, he says, there would be no reason for them to worry about behaving morally. They could simply act to satisfy their desires. This idea scandalizes Miusov and troubles Dmitri. Zosima gently notes that Ivan himself is beset with doubt and advocates positions he does not entirely believe, merely to toy with his own despair.

As the debate enters a lull, Fyodor Pavlovich begins to criticize and insult Dmitri. He accuses his son of dealing falsely with his fiancée, Katerina, and deserting her after falling in love with another woman, Grushenka. As the others look on in embarrassment, Dmitri gives an angry reply that helps explain the conflict between Dmitri and his father: Dmitri says that Fyodor Pavlovich is jealous because Fyodor Pavlovich also lusts after Grushenka and has made a fool of himself trying to win her heart. Dmitri says that Fyodor Pavlovich has even tried to convince Grushenka to collaborate with him to send Dmitri to prison. The men go on shouting at one another, until suddenly Zosima stands up. He walks over to Dmitri and kneels before him. Then, wordlessly, he leaves the room. The others are baffled by this gesture. As they prepare to have lunch with the Father Superior, Fyodor Pavlovich leaves in a huff.

SUMMARY—CHAPTER 7: A SEMINARIST-CAREERIST
When Zosima leaves the room after kneeling before Dmitri, Alyosha follows close behind him. When Alyosha catches up, Zosima tells him that he wants Alyosha to leave the monastery, rejoin the world, and even find a wife. Alyosha is upset, but Zosima, smiling, tells Alyosha that his path lies outside the monastery. Zosima says that he has great faith in Alyosha, and then sends him away.

SUMMARY & ANALYSIS

Alyosha walks with Rakitin to meet the Father Superior, and they discuss the meaning of Zosima's strange departure. Rakitin says that the Karamazov dynasty is coming to a violent end, for the Karamazovs are all "sensualists" who only love women and money. He says that Dmitri has indeed abandoned his fiancée for Grushenka, and that Ivan is now trying to steal Dmitri's cast-off fiancée, with Dmitri's consent, while Fyodor Pavlovich chases after Dmitri's mistress. Rakitin says that Zosima understands that this drama can only end in bloodshed, and that he bowed to Dmitri so that, after the tragedy occurs, people will think Zosima had foreseen it. Rakitin goes on insulting the Karamazovs and Grushenka, even saying that Grushenka wishes to seduce Alyosha, until Alyosha asks whether Grushenka is not one of Rakitin's relatives. Rakitin, angry and embarrassed, denies this claim.

SUMMARY — CHAPTER 8: SCANDAL

Fyodor Pavlovich creates another scene before leaving the monastery. He angrily bursts in on the luncheon at the Father Superior's and launches into a long, vulgar tirade about the idiocy and hypocrisy of monastic life. Fyodor finally leaves, and as Ivan unhappily loads him into a carriage, he shouts back at Alyosha to leave the monastery and come home at once. The carriage drives away, and Fyodor begins contemplating the cognac he will have when they return home.

ANALYSIS — BOOK II: AN INAPPROPRIATE GATHERING, CHAPTERS 5–8

Ivan's argument with the monks in Chapters 5 and 6 provides an approach to the world's problems that contrasts with the active love promoted by Zosima in the previous section. Unlike Zosima, who emphasizes the role of the individual conscience, Ivan proposes sweeping social changes designed to promote a specific outcome. While Zosima believes that every person should strive to do good, Ivan argues that civilization should erase the distinction between church and state in order to reduce criminality.

Ivan's position differs from Zosima's in three specific ways. First, Ivan is interested in abstract conceptions of society and large groups of people, while Zosima is interested in the experience of the individual. Zosima proposes a way of life that, if everyone were to follow it, would make a better world, and Ivan proposes a change in the order of the world that, if enacted, would possibly make a better life for individuals. This difference is understandable given Ivan's and Zosima's own characteristics. Zosima is capable of loving human beings on an individual level, while Ivan is only capable of loving humanity in the abstract. Second, Zosima conceives of religion as a positive force, but Ivan believes it is negative. Zosima's approach to religion is to suggest ways that the individual can act to do good, while Ivan's is to suggest ways that religion can prevent the individual from doing evil. Because Zosima believes people are naturally loving and positive, he emphasizes the good that people can do for one another. Because Ivan believes people are naturally suspicious and negative, he emphasizes the evil that people must be prevented from doing to one another.

The third difference between Zosima's and Ivan's arguments is their level of sincerity. Zosima wholeheartedly believes what he says, whereas Ivan argues from a detached, academic standpoint. Ivan does believe that powerful ecclesiastical courts would improve society. But he does not believe in God, making his desire for a religious society seem perplexingly out of line with his real beliefs. Nonetheless, Ivan thinks that religious courts would be most effective in controlling the masses, even if religion itself is false. The fact that Zosima is able to see Ivan's religious doubt even as Ivan argues for increased religious authority shows Zosima's penetrating understanding of human nature.

These chapters represent the conflict between faith and doubt as a struggle between simple love for humanity and complicated theorizing about humanity. Zosima and Ivan both argue convincingly for their ideas, but Zosima's simple faith is more impressive than Ivan's highly complex doubt. Dostoevsky's treatment of philosophical concepts in this chapter is similar to his treatment of them in the rest of the novel. Dostoevsky frequently makes compelling abstract cases for two sides of an argument, and then, through the example of the characters' behavior, indicates the superiority of love, faith, and goodness.

Zosima's enigmatic action when he kneels before Dmitri is open to a variety of interpretations. Zosima is able to understand other people's minds because his faith is logical and clearheaded. His kneeling before Dmitri indicates his understanding of something that no other character can see yet: that Dmitri, deep down, is a good man who will be forced to suffer before he can be redeemed. The narrative suggests that Zosima's insight is vastly superior to the sly theorizing of Rakitin in Chapter 7—Zosima is able to predict Dmitri's real future, whereas the rational Rakitin predicts that Dmitri will come to a violent end. In this way, Zosima's bow foreshadows Dmitri's eventual fate. It also foreshadows a number of similarly enigmatic gestures made throughout the novel in moments of moral conflict, including Christ kissing the Grand Inquisitor and Alyosha kissing Ivan in Book V.

Ivan's argument that the entire notion of morality is dependent on the idea that the soul is immortal has a direct bearing on Fyodor Pavlovich's character. If, as Ivan proposes, the idea of good and evil is dependent upon the existence of God, then Fyodor Pavlovich's gross sensuality is a perfectly logical way for him to behave, as he does not believe in God. All of Fyodor Pavlovich's morally questionable actions are irrelevant if morality is only a tool for securing a comfortable afterlife. Ivan himself seems to understand that Fyodor Pavlovich lives the logical extension of Ivan's own beliefs. This relationship between the two characters explains the simultaneous love and hatred Ivan feels toward his father. Ivan hates Fyodor Pavlovich because Ivan dislikes the idea that his argument about morality could justify such an abhorrent figure as Fyodor. But Ivan must tolerate Fyodor Pavlovich, because criticizing him would undermine his argument.

BOOK III: THE SENSUALISTS, CHAPTERS 1–11

SUMMARY—CHAPTER 1: IN THE SERVANT'S QUARTERS

The narrator tells the story of Fyodor Pavlovich Karamazov's servant Grigory, who briefly cares for each of the three Karamazov brothers when they are young. Grigory's wife gives birth to a child with six fingers. The child dies two weeks after it is born. The night Grigory buries it, his wife hears a baby crying in the distance. When Grigory goes to investigate, he discovers a newborn child lying next to a young girl, who has just given birth and is dying.

SUMMARY—CHAPTER 2: STINKING LIZAVETA

The girl whom Grigory sees giving birth is Lizaveta, often called "stinking Lizaveta." Lizaveta is extremely slow-witted and cannot talk. The people of the town are appalled that someone has seduced this helpless young girl, and they agree that the only man vile enough to do so is Fyodor Pavlovich. Grigory and his wife adopt the baby, and Fyodor Pavlovich names him Smerdyakov.

SUMMARY—CHAPTER 3:
THE CONFESSION OF AN ARDENT HEART. IN VERSE

Alyosha leaves the monastery, as he has been ordered to do by both Zosima and his father. A wealthy gentlewoman friend of the Karamazovs, Madame Khokhlakov, has given Alyosha a note from Katerina,

Dmitri's abandoned fiancée, asking him to visit her. Somewhat nervous about the prospect, Alyosha sets off for Katerina's house before returning to his father's. Alyosha assumes that he will not see Ivan or Dmitri at Katerina's house, though he thinks he would like to talk to Dmitri before he sees Katerina. Taking a shortcut to Katerina's house, he is surprised by Dmitri, who intercepts him on the path.

SUMMARY — CHAPTER 4:
THE CONFESSION OF AN ARDENT HEART. IN ANECDOTES

Dmitri relates his history with Katerina to Alyosha. Dmitri first met Katerina when she was the daughter of the commanding officer of a camp where Dmitri was stationed as a soldier. Katerina ignored Dmitri until he attempted to trick her into sleeping with him by offering 4,500 rubles to pay off an obligation of her father's. As he began to put his plan into motion, he was suddenly overcome with self-disgust, and, looking at the beautiful, innocent Katerina, decided to give her the money without even trying to seduce her. When she inherited a large amount of money from a relative, she offered to marry Dmitri. But when they returned to Fyodor Pavlovich's town, Dmitri fell swiftly for Grushenka. He even stole 3,000 rubles from Katerina in order to finance his debauchery with Grushenka.

SUMMARY — CHAPTER 5: THE CONFESSION OF AN ARDENT HEART. "HEELS UP"

Dmitri asks Alyosha to tell Katerina that the engagement is officially off. He also asks Alyosha to procure 3,000 rubles from their father so that he can pay Katerina back and ease his conscience. Dmitri knows that Fyodor Pavlovich has 3,000 rubles readily available because Fyodor Pavlovich has assembled that very sum of money in the hopes of buying Grushenka's affections.

SUMMARY — CHAPTER 6: SMERDYAKOV

Alyosha goes to his father's house, where he finds his father drinking. Ivan sits by Fyodor Pavlovich disapprovingly. Smerdyakov and Grigory are arguing, and Ivan and Fyodor Pavlovich are listening in on their argument. Smerdyakov is a sullen and gloomy young man who despises everyone in the house, including his adoptive parents. He works as a cook for Fyodor Pavlovich. Most of the household considers him a responsible person despite his churlish attitude, because once, when Fyodor Pavlovich lost 300 rubles in a drunken stupor, Smerdyakov found and returned the money to him.

SUMMARY — CHAPTER 7: DISPUTATION

Grigory and Smerdyakov are arguing over whether it is morally acceptable to renounce one's faith in God if doing so would save one's life. Smerdyakov says that it is, because no one has perfect faith. He says that no one has faith enough to believe that, if he asked a mountain to move, God would move the mountain. Therefore, Smerdyakov says, no one should die for the faith that he does have. He says that a person who renounces his faith to save his life can repent for his sin later. Though he is arguing with Grigory, he seems to be directing most of his attention to Ivan, and he seems to hope that Ivan will approve of his reasoning.

SUMMARY — CHAPTER 8: OVER THE COGNAC

Fyodor Pavlovich is soon bored with his servants' quarrel, and he dismisses them. He asks Ivan about his religious belief, and Ivan says that he does not believe in God or in the immortality of the soul. Alyosha defends religion, claiming that God does exist and that the soul is immortal. Fyodor Pavlovich is quickly bored of this debate and instead of furthering it, he begins to taunt Alyosha about his mother. He attacks her religious faith and describes her seizures, and Alyosha grows so upset with this attack that he has a seizure himself. Ivan angrily reminds Fyodor Pavlovich that he and Alyosha have the same mother—Fyodor Pavlovich has forgotten that they are both the children of his second marriage. Suddenly, Dmitri comes into the room, screaming at his father and insisting that Grushenka is hidden in Fyodor Pavlovich's house.

SUMMARY — CHAPTER 9: THE SENSUALISTS

Dmitri runs through the rooms trying to find Grushenka, and when Fyodor Pavlovich accuses him of stealing money, Dmitri throws his father to the ground, threatens to kill him, and runs out of the house. Alyosha and Ivan tend to Fyodor Pavlovich's wounds and put him to bed.

SUMMARY — CHAPTER 10: THE TWO TOGETHER

Alyosha visits Katerina at Madame Khokhlakov's house and is surprised to find that Grushenka is also there. Grushenka has just promised Katerina that she is going to leave Dmitri for a former lover, and Katerina will have him back soon. Katerina is grateful and overjoyed, but when she tells Alyosha what has happened, Grushenka insults her and says that she may decide to stay with Dmitri after all. On his way out of the house, Alyosha is stopped by a maid, who gives him a letter from Lise.

SUMMARY—CHAPTER 11: ONE MORE RUINED REPUTATION

As he returns to the monastery, Alyosha is again stopped by Dmitri, who laughs at the report of Grushenka's behavior. Suddenly remorseful, Dmitri then tells Alyosha that he is consumed by self-disgust. At the monastery that night, Alyosha learns that Zosima's health is rapidly deteriorating, and Zosima is near death. Alyosha decides to remain with Zosima, whom he loves like a father, instead of returning to help with his family's conflict. He reads Lise's letter, which contains a confession of her love for him. She writes that she hopes to marry Alyosha one day. Alyosha laughs happily, says a prayer for all his troubled loved ones, and, after such an eventful day, falls into a deep sleep.

ANALYSIS: BOOK III: THE SENSUALISTS, CHAPTERS 1–11

The Brothers Karamazov is a systematically ordered novel. Each of the story's twelve books chronicles a specific phase of its development and approaches its narrative from a specific angle. Book I gives the novel's background, detailing Fyodor Pavlovich Karamazov's past and the three brothers' childhoods. Book II deals with the meeting at the monastery, outlines some of the novel's major philosophical conflicts, and introduces us to the source of conflict between Fyodor Pavlovich and Dmitri—their rivalry for Grushenka. Book III finally introduces the town in which the main portion of the novel's action takes place and presents a firsthand view of the situation between the main characters, as opposed to the secondhand views presented by Fyodor Pavlovich, Rakitin, and Dmitri in Book II. Significantly, Book III presents the narration from Alyosha's perspective for an extended period of time. Although the narrator describes Alyosha as the "hero" of the novel, he has been only a minor participant in the story so far.

One of *The Brothers Karamazov*'s major arguments is that Alyosha's nonjudgmental love of humanity improves the lives of the people with whom he interacts. Specifically, he bridges the communication gap between Dmitri and Katerina, provides hope and love to Lise, and tends to Fyodor Pavlovich after Dmitri attacks him. Dostoevsky repeatedly shows how Alyosha is impervious to the conflicts and built-up hatreds of the other characters, and how his soothing, relieving presence encourages peace and resolution between them. Zosima's understanding of Alyosha's capability to do good is presumably what leads him to send Alyosha out of the monastery and back into the world. Although that decision is a mystery in Book II, in Book III it becomes clear that Zosima's motivation is to allow Alyosha to do good in the world. Alyosha works to bring Zosima's ideas to fruition in the real world and exemplifies the novel's moral standpoint. Alyosha represents not only the simple, loving religious faith described by Zosima, but also the power of that faith to do actual good in the world.

Dmitri represents a combination of the ideas that drive Alyosha and Fyodor Pavlovich. He has Fyodor Pavlovich's inclination toward Epicurean sensuality and Alyosha's inclination toward morality and faith. When Rakitin accuses Dmitri of having the same sensualist greed and lust as Fyodor Pavlovich, Dmitri reveals his deep-seated disgust with his own behavior. The fact that he hates himself for treating Katerina poorly makes him morally superior to Fyodor Pavlovich. It is difficult for us to imagine Fyodor Pavlovich feeling similar remorse. Additionally, the story about Dmitri's abandoned attempt to blackmail Katerina into sleeping with him reveals a level of moral concern that is also lacking in Fyodor Pavlovich. Dmitri begins to emerge as the person Zosima recognizes him to be from the beginning: a troubled, confused young man, driven to sin by the power of his passions, but struggling to live by his conscience.

The story of the birth of Smerdyakov, chronicled in the early chapters of Book III, reveals the extent of Fyodor Pavlovich's disregard for moral laws. His seduction and possible rape of a helpless idiot girl, combined with his reprehensible treatment of the resulting child, reveal the worst consequences of a life lived with no conception of good and evil. This depraved existence is the sort of life Ivan unhappily sees as the logical course of action for a man who does not believe in God. The twisted, unpleasant Smerdyakov, cursed with epilepsy, becomes a symbol of Fyodor Pavlovich's deformed life, the illegitimate son's mean temperament and unhealthy body resulting directly from his father's wicked behavior. The contrast between Alyosha and Fyodor Pavlovich illustrates the superiority of a life of faith and love over a life of doubt and selfishness.

BOOK IV: STRAINS, CHAPTERS 1–7

SUMMARY — CHAPTER 1: FATHER FERAPONT

Zosima, realizing that he will soon die, summons a group of students and friends to his side to have one last conversation about faith, love, and goodness. As he speaks, he emphasizes the importance of actively loving mankind, and of carrying universal love into all dealings with other people. He also discourages his listeners from being judgmental, saying that every person on Earth shares the blame for the sins of every other person.

As Alyosha leaves Zosima's bedside, he reflects on his elder's impending death, and thinks that surely God would not let such a wise man die without marking his death with a spectacular miracle of some sort. Alyosha is certain that everyone in the monastery feels the same way, with the possible exception of the dour Father Ferapont, Zosima's enemy and an advocate of a harsh and ascetic form of piety that bears little resemblance to Zosima's warmhearted doctrine of love and forgiveness.

Zosima calls Alyosha back to his cell. He asks him again to leave the monastery in order to help his family and to do good in the town. This time, Alyosha agrees to do so.

SUMMARY — CHAPTER 2: AT HIS FATHER'S

Alyosha returns home, where he encounters Fyodor Pavlovich scheming about the future. Fyodor Pavlovich tells Alyosha that he plans to live for many years and intends to remain a sensualist until he dies, when his only lover will be death. He says that he will eventually be too old to attract young women, however, and so he will need a great deal of money to lure them into his bed. He also insinuates that Ivan is trying to seduce Katerina in order to make Dmitri marry Grushenka. Should Ivan be successful, Fyodor Pavlovich says, Fyodor Pavlovich himself would be unable to marry Grushenka, and Ivan would ensure that his part of the Karamazov fortune would not be left to Fyodor Pavlovich's new wife. Fyodor Pavlovich recognizes his own wickedness, and Alyosha replies that he is not evil; he is just twisted.

SUMMARY — CHAPTER 3: HE GETS INVOLVED WITH
SCHOOLBOYS

Alyosha sets off for Madame Khokhlakov's house. On the way, he sees a group of young bullies throwing rocks at a frail boy, who, despite his disadvantages, ferociously hurls rocks back. When the boy runs away, Alyosha runs after him, hoping to talk with him, but when Alyosha catches him, the boy hits him with a rock and bites his finger. The boy runs away again, leaving Alyosha confused and troubled, wondering what could cause such savage behavior in such a young boy.

SUMMARY — CHAPTER 4: AT THE KHOKHLAKOVS'

At Madame Khokhlakov's, Alyosha is surprised to learn that Ivan is already there, visiting Katerina. The two are upstairs, and before

Alyosha joins them, he asks Madame Khokhlakov for a bandage for his hand. When she goes in search of supplies with which to tend his wound, Alyosha is accosted by Lise, who insists that he give her back the love letter she wrote him. She says that it was merely a joke. Alyosha refuses to give the letter back, saying that he fell for the joke and that he did not bring the letter with him.

SUMMARY—CHAPTER 5: STRAIN IN THE DRAWING-ROOM

Alyosha goes upstairs to talk to Ivan and Katerina. To Alyosha's eyes, Ivan and Katerina are obviously in love, but they torment one another and themselves by inventing moral barriers to keep them apart. Katerina tells Alyosha that she intends to stay loyal to Dmitri, even if he decides to abandon her and marry Grushenka. Ivan says that he thinks her commitment to Dmitri is the right decision. Frustrated, Alyosha tries to make them see that they are only hurting themselves by refusing to acknowledge their love for one another. Ivan admits that he loves Katerina, but says that he thinks she needs to have Dmitri in her life. He says that he has decided to leave for Moscow the next day, and says good-bye.

After Ivan leaves, Katerina tells Alyosha a story about an old captain who once provoked Dmitri's wrath. Dmitri beat him badly in front of the captain's young son, who begged him to spare his father. Katerina asks Alyosha to take 200 rubles to the captain to help make up for Dmitri's violence, and Alyosha agrees.

SUMMARY—CHAPTER 6: STRAIN IN THE COTTAGE

Alyosha travels to the poor captain's hovel, where he discovers to his surprise that the captain's son, Ilyusha, is the same young boy who bit him. He realizes that Ilyusha attacked him because he is the brother of the man who assaulted Ilyusha's father.

SUMMARY—CHAPTER 7: AND IN THE FRESH AIR

The captain is at first overjoyed at the prospect of 200 rubles. But after some consideration, he proudly throws the money to the ground, explaining that if he accepted it, his son would never be able to admire or respect him. Alyosha sets out to return the money to Katerina.

ANALYSIS: BOOK IV: STRAINS, CHAPTERS 1–7

Alyosha and Zosima are extremely similar characters. Alyosha possesses Zosima's ability to ascertain a great deal about a person's inner self through simple observation. Alyosha also practices Zosima's lesson of not judging other people. Finally, Alyosha's interaction with his father shows his ability to feel empathy for people's shortcomings while at the same time refraining from apologizing for their failings. His willingness to declare that his father is twisted illustrates his honesty and integrity, as well as his intricate understanding of human character—Alyosha draws a distinction between evil and immorality. His immediate understanding of Ivan and Katerina's relationship, his respect for the captain, and his sense that there is more to Ilyusha than violence and hostility all attest to his ability to quickly understand other people, a skill he learns from Zosima. Dostoevsky links this capability to moral purity throughout the novel, implying that the more honest and simple a person's faith is, the more easily that person will understand fellow human beings.

The conflict between faith and doubt that pervades *The Brothers Karamazov* shows the detrimental effects of skepticism on the human character. For Dostoevsky, faith essentially represents a positive commitment to the truth, while doubt represents the suspicion that what poses as the truth is really a lie. As a result, a religious man like Zosima is capable of immediately perceiving the truth about others, whereas an irreligious man like Fyodor Pavlovich is consumed with suspicion and mistrust. Fyodor Pavlovich illustrates this difference in his suspicion that Ivan's attempt to seduce Katerina is actually a plot to keep Grushenka from marrying Fyodor Pavlovich. Fyodor Pavlovich himself is so dishonest that he assumes everyone around him is equally dishonest, and as a result, his lack of self-respect translates into as a lack of respect for the rest of humanity. This breakdown is what Zosima means when he says that the man who is dishonest with himself is incapable of love.

Whereas Alyosha and Zosima love humankind because of their faith, the doubt that Ivan and Katerina feel makes them fatalistic. They see human nature as unchangeable, and therefore view people's lives as predetermined. Ivan sees Katerina's need to humiliate herself before Dmitri as a necessary part of her personality, and with that knowledge, he is paralyzed to act on his love for her, which he pridefully scorns as irrelevant. Katerina, who has been deeply hurt by Dmitri, has a corresponding sense that other people will disappoint her and cause her pain, and this sense manifests itself in her haughty desire to be made a martyr by the inevitable betrayals of those around her. She is unable to accept happiness as a possible outcome in her life, and as a result, she embraces humiliation and pain. Thus, she is just as paralyzed as Ivan, similarly unable to act on her feelings. In both of their cases, Dostoevsky shows how a kernel of doubt can spread through a person's character, transforming itself into a defensive pride that renders the person unable to be honest, happy, or capable of pursuing happiness.

BOOK V: PRO AND CONTRA, CHAPTERS 1–4

> *Listen: if everyone must suffer, in order to buy eternal harmony with their suffering, pray tell me what have children got to do with it? It's quite incomprehensible why they should have to suffer, and why they should buy harmony with their suffering.*
>
> *(See* QUOTATIONS, *p. 75)*

SUMMARY — CHAPTER 1: A BETROTHAL

Back at Madame Khokhlakov's house, Alyosha discovers that Katerina has come down with a fever, apparently due to her intense humiliation over Dmitri's decision to leave her. Alyosha talks with Lise and tells her about his failure to convince the captain to take Katerina's money. Deeply moved by Alyosha's gentle wisdom, Lise suddenly admits that her love letter was sincere. Alyosha also loves Lise, and the two young people begin to plan their marriage. Alyosha also confesses that he deceived Lise about the letter. He refused to give it back to her, not because he did not have it with him, as he claimed, but because it was too important to him to give up.

As Alyosha leaves, Madame Khokhlakov stops him. She has listened in on his conversation with Lise, and says that she is bitterly unhappy at the thought of his marriage to Lise. Madame Khokhlakov implies that Lise has been increasingly unreliable and difficult lately. When the daughter marries, she says, the mother has nothing to look forward to but death. Alyosha tries to calm her by telling her that the marriage will not take place for at least another year and a half, but when she presses him to show her Lise's letter, he refuses outright.

SUMMARY — CHAPTER 2: SMERDYAKOV WITH A GUITAR

Alyosha thinks about Dmitri's violent and passionate behavior, and decides to try to help his brother rather than return to Zosima's bedside in the monastery as he longs to do. Alyosha notes that Dmitri seems to be avoiding him, so Alyosha decides to stake out the gazebo that he knows Dmitri often visits to watch for Grushenka. There, Alyosha overhears Smerdyakov playing a guitar and singing a song for the housekeeper's daughter. Alyosha tentatively interrupts this scene and asks Smerdyakov if he knows where Dmitri has gone. Smerdyakov says that Dmitri has gone to meet Ivan at a restaurant.

SUMMARY—CHAPTER 3: THE BROTHERS GET ACQUAINTED

When Alyosha arrives at the restaurant, he finds Ivan sitting at a table alone. Ivan asks Alyosha to join him and says he has begun to admire him and would like to get to know him better. Alyosha is worried about what will happen to Fyodor Pavlovich and Dmitri if Ivan leaves for Moscow, but Ivan firmly declares that what happens to the others is not his responsibility. He says, in fact, that it was Fyodor Pavlovich's repulsiveness that caused him to come to this restaurant in the first place, simply to escape.

SUMMARY—CHAPTER 4: REBELLION

The two brothers begin to discuss questions of God's existence and the immortality of the soul. Ivan says that, in his heart, he has not rejected God, but that at the same time he feels himself unable to accept God or the world that God has created. Ivan says that he can love humanity in the abstract, but that, when he meets individual men and women, he finds it impossible to love them. Moreover, he is deeply troubled by the injustice of suffering on Earth. He asks Alyosha how a just God could permit the suffering of children, creatures too young even to have sinned. He says that to love such a God would be the equivalent of a tortured man choosing to love his torturer. When Alyosha is troubled by Ivan's position, Ivan asks him if he could accept even a perfect world in which the perfection depended on the suffering of an innocent creature. Alyosha reminds Ivan of the sacrifice of Christ, and Ivan, insisting that he has not forgotten Christ, recites a prose poem, called *The Grand Inquisitor*, that he wrote some time ago.

SUMMARY & ANALYSIS

ANALYSIS—BOOK V: PRO AND CONTRA, CHAPTERS 1–4

Lise is portrayed as a character poised between the two philosophical poles of the novel: the love represented by Alyosha and the despair represented by Ivan. Lise's gleefully mischievous behavior in the early part of the novel is actually the early onset of what finally becomes a wild, temperamental capriciousness. She struggles to be happy, but, as is clear from her increasingly antagonistic behavior toward her mother, she is beginning to distrust the authority figures in her life and to feel frustrated with the shortcomings of the world around her. She reacts to her inner turmoil with wild mood swings and displays of extreme affection and extreme hatred. In this way, Lise is linked to the "shriekers" described in Books I and II, women who are so unable to cope with the horrors of the world that they collapse into hysteria, and thus serve as symbols of the despair that besets those who share the anguished doubt embodied by Ivan. In this part of the novel, Lise seizes on Alyosha as a possible source of salvation. But while she admires his blithe faith, she is unable to share it, and she eventually succumbs to a petulant, spiteful despair. Though this scene seems happy, the seeds of Lise's downfall are already apparent in the way that she rebels against her mother, in the extremity of her emotional displays, and in the way she oscillates between admitting and hiding her love for Alyosha.

Ivan's dinner conversation with Alyosha adds a new level of complexity to the novel's exploration of religion and spirituality. The novel does not simplistically suggest that belief in God brings unmitigated happiness while doubt brings unmitigated suffering, and the brothers' dinner conversation provides the rationale behind the idea that not believing in God is more reasonable and compassionate than believing in him. Through his description of the unjust suffering of children and of the general misery of mankind's situation on Earth, Ivan presents the strongest case against religion in the novel. Ivan's dilemma mirrors the biblical dilemma of Job, who asked how a loving God could allow mankind to endure injustice and misery for no apparent reason. Ivan cannot understand why young children would be made to suffer under a loving God. In rejecting outright the explanation that God's ways are too mysterious for mankind to comprehend, Ivan illustrates the depth of his commitment to rational coherence. He can only believe in a God who is rational like the human beings he created, and he thinks that a truly loving God would have made the universe comprehensible to mankind. As such, Ivan's religious doubt is slightly different from atheism, because Ivan says that if God does indeed exist, he is not good or just. The problem is not resolvable. Either no God exists, or a God exists who is the equivalent of a torturer. This problem is the ultimate source of Ivan's despair. Ivan's understanding of the world means that mankind is alone in the universe and that Fyodor Pavlovich's revolting attitude toward life is acceptable and even logical. If this is not the case, then God himself must be a heartless tyrant.

Book V: Pro and Contra, Chapter 5: The Grand Inquisitor

[N]othing has ever been more insufferable for man than freedom!

(See QUOTATIONS, *p. 76*)

Summary

Ivan explains his prose poem, "The Grand Inquisitor." In a town in Spain, in the sixteenth century, Christ arrives, apparently reborn on Earth. As he walks through the streets, the people gather about him, staring. He begins to heal the sick, but his ministrations are interrupted by the arrival of a powerful cardinal who orders his guards to arrest Christ. Late that night, this cardinal, the Grand Inquisitor, visits Christ's cell and explains why he has taken him prisoner and why he cannot allow Christ to perform his works. Throughout the Grand Inquisitor's lecture, Christ listens silently.

The Grand Inquisitor tells Christ that he cannot allow him to do his work on Earth, because his work is at odds with the work of the Church. The Inquisitor reminds Christ of the time, recorded in the Bible, when the Devil presented him with three temptations, each of which he rejected. The Grand Inquisitor says that by rejecting these three temptations, he guaranteed that human beings would have free will. Free will, he says, is a devastating, impossible burden for mankind. Christ gave humanity the freedom to choose whether or not to follow him, but almost no one is strong enough to be faithful, and those who are not will be damned forever. The Grand Inquisitor says that Christ should have given people no choice, and instead taken power and given people security instead of freedom. That way, the same people who were too weak to follow Christ to begin with would still be damned, but at least they could have happiness and security on Earth, rather than the impossible burden of moral freedom. The Grand Inquisitor says that the Church has now undertaken to correct Christ's mistake. The Church is taking away freedom of choice and replacing it with security. Thus, the Grand Inquisitor must keep Christ in prison, because if Christ were allowed to go free, he might undermine the Church's work to lift the burden of free will from mankind.

The first temptation Christ rejected was bread. Hungry after his forty days of fasting, Christ was confronted by Satan, who told him that if he were really the son of God, he could turn a stone to bread and satisfy his hunger. Christ refused, replying that man should not live by bread, but by the word of God. The Grand Inquisitor says that most people are too weak to live by the word of God when they are hungry. Christ should have taken the bread and offered mankind freedom from hunger instead of freedom of choice.

The second temptation was to perform a miracle. Satan placed Christ upon a pinnacle in Jerusalem and told him to prove that he was the messiah by throwing himself off it. If Christ were really God's son, the angels would bear him up and not allow him to die. Christ refused, telling Satan that he could not tempt God. Beaten, Satan departed. But the Grand Inquisitor says that Christ should have given people a miracle, for most people need to see the miraculous in order to be content in their religious faith. Man needs a supernatural being to worship, and Christ refused to appear as one.

The third temptation was power. Satan showed Christ all the kingdoms in the world, and offered him control of them all. Christ refused. The Grand Inquisitor says that Christ should have taken the power, but since he did not, the Church has now has to take it in his name, in order to convince men to give up their free will in favor of their security.

The Grand Inquisitor tells Christ that it was Satan, and not Christ, who was in the right during this exchange. He says that ever since the Church took over the Roman Empire, it has been secretly performing the work of Satan, not because it is evil, but because it seeks the best and most secure order for mankind.

As the Grand Inquisitor finishes his indictment of Christ, Christ walks up to the old man and kisses him gently on the lips. The Grand Inquisitor suddenly sets Christ free, but tells him never to return again.

As Ivan finishes his story, he worries that Alyosha will be disturbed by the idea that if there is no God, there are no moral limitations on man's behavior. But Alyosha leans forward and kisses Ivan on the lips. Ivan, moved, replies that Alyosha has stolen that action from his poem. Ivan and Alyosha leave the restaurant and split up. Ivan begins walking home and Alyosha walks to the monastery where Zosima is dying.

ANALYSIS

The story of the Grand Inquisitor strongly resembles a biblical parable, the kind of story that Christ tells in the New Testament to illustrate a philosophical point. Both Ivan's story and Christ's stories use a fictional narrative to address a deep philosophical concern and are open to various interpretations. The similarity between Ivan's story and Christ's stories illustrates the uneasy relationship between Ivan and religion. At the same time that Ivan rejects religion's ability to effectively guide human life, he relies on many of its principles in forming his own philosophical system. Like Christ, Ivan is deeply concerned with understanding the way we define what is right and what is wrong, and with understanding how morality guides human actions. However, Ivan ultimately rejects both Christ's and God's existence, as he cannot accept a supreme being with absolute power who would nonetheless allow the suffering that occurs on Earth.

The story also implicitly brings up a new point with regard to Ivan's argument about expanding the power of ecclesiastical courts. By setting his story in sixteenth-century Spain, where ecclesiastical courts were at the height of their power to try and punish criminals, Ivan asks what verdict such a court would have reached in judging Christ's life. Since Christian religions teach that Christ lived a sinless life, presumably an ecclesiastical court would have been unable to find Christ guilty of any sin. However, the fact that Ivan's court finds Christ guilty of sins against mankind illustrates the difference between Ivan's religious beliefs and his beliefs in the efficacy of ecclesiastical courts. He sees the courts as an effective way to guide human action, but not necessarily as a way to induce men to believe more strongly in God or religion.

The conflict between free will and security further illustrates the reasons for Ivan's dissent from Christianity. The fundamental difference between Christ's point of view and that of the Grand Inquisitor is the value that each of them places on freedom and comfort. Christ's responses to the three temptations emphasize the importance of man's ability to choose between right and wrong, while the Inquisitor's interpretation of Christ's actions emphasizes the greater value of living a comfortable life in which the right path has already been chosen by someone else.

The assumption at the heart of the Inquisitor's case is that Christ's resistance of Satan's temptations is meant to provide a symbolic example for the rest of mankind. The Inquisitor interprets the rejection of the temptations as Christ's argument that humanity must reject certain securities: comfort, represented by bread; power and the safety that power brings, represented by the kingdoms; and superstition, represented by the miracle. The Inquisitor believes that Christ's example places an impossible burden on mankind, which is inherently too weak to use its free will to find salvation. Effectively, the Inquisitor argues, the only option is for people to lead sinful lives ending in damnation. The Inquisitor's Church, which is allied with Satan, seeks to provide people with stability and security in their lives, even if by doing so it ensures that they will be damned in the afterlife.

Ivan's story presents the Inquisitor, a man who considers himself an ally of Satan, as an admirable human being, acting against God but with humanity's best interest at heart. Ivan does not believe that God acts in the best interest of mankind, but the implication that human nature is so weak that people are better off succumbing to the power of Satan is a radical response to the problem of free will. Ivan's attitude stems from the psychology of doubt. Ivan's overriding skepticism makes it impossible for him to see anything but the bad side of human nature. As a result, he believes that people would be better off under the thumb of even a fraudulent religious authority rather than making their own decisions. Even though his argument is pessimistic, his reasoning is compelling.

Just as Alyosha is unable to offer a satisfactory response to Ivan's critique of God, Christ says nothing during the Inquisitor's critique of him, one of several parallels between Alyosha and Christ during this chapter. But Christ's enigmatic kiss on the Inquisitor's lips after his indictment completely changes the tenor of the scene. Recalling Zosima's bow before Dmitri at the monastery in Book I, the kiss represents an overriding act of love and forgiveness so innate that it can only be expressed wordlessly. On its deepest level, it defies explanation. The power of faith and love, Dostoevsky implies, is rooted in mystery—not simply in the empty and easily digestible idea that God's will is too complex for people to understand, but in a resonant, active, unanswerable profundity. The kiss cannot overcome a logical argument, but at the same time there is no logical argument that can overcome the kiss. It represents the triumph of love and faith, on their own terms, over rational skepticism. In having Ivan end his poem on a note of such deep and moving ambiguity, Dostoevsky has his major opponent of religion acknowledge the power of faith, just as Dostoevsky himself, a proponent of faith, has used Ivan to acknowledge the power of doubt. Alyosha's kiss for Ivan indicates how well the young Alyosha understands the problems of faith and doubt in a world characterized by free will, and just how committed his own will is to the positive goodness of faith.

BOOK V: PRO AND CONTRA, CHAPTERS 6–7

SUMMARY—CHAPTER 6: A RATHER OBSCURE ONE FOR THE MOMENT

Since arriving at his father's house, Ivan has spent a great deal of time discussing religion and philosophy with Smerdyakov. But Ivan dislikes Smerdyakov, and when he returns home at night, he dreads the possibility of seeing him. At Fyodor Pavlovich's house, Ivan sees Smerdyakov sitting in the yard. Ivan intends to walk by Smerdyakov, or even insult him, but to his own surprise he finds himself stopping and asking about their father.

Smerdyakov says that he is worried about Fyodor Pavlovich because Dmitri now knows the secret signs that Grushenka and Fyodor Pavlovich have agreed upon if Grushenka ever decides to be Fyodor Pavlovich's lover. If Grushenka comes to Fyodor Pavlovich, Dmitri will know about it, and Smerdyakov worries that there would be no one to defend Fyodor Pavlovich from Dmitri's rage. Smerdyakov says that Grigory and his wife have begun to take a medicine that makes them sleep deeply, and he is afraid that his own nervousness will cause him to have an epileptic seizure.

SUMMARY — CHAPTER 7: "IT'S ALWAYS INTERESTING TO TALK WITH AN INTELLIGENT MAN"

Ivan suspects that Smerdyakov has told Dmitri about Grushenka's secret signs specifically to place Fyodor Pavlovich in danger. But Ivan is determined to leave for Moscow as planned the following morning, even though Smerdyakov asks him to go to a city that is not so far away.

The next morning, Fyodor Pavlovich too asks Ivan not to leave for Moscow. Instead, he wants Ivan to go to a nearby village to sell a plot of wood on Fyodor Pavlovich's behalf. Ivan reluctantly agrees. After he leaves, Smerdyakov falls down a staircase and has the epileptic seizure he has feared. He is confined to his bed, leaving Fyodor Pavlovich alone. The old man waits gleefully for Grushenka, whom he is certain will come to him tonight.

ANALYSIS

These chapters foreshadow Smerdyakov's eventual murder of Fyodor Pavlovich. Although Smerdyakov appears to be worried about Fyodor Pavlovich, his concern only serves to mask his deeper malice, and everything he does in this chapter lays the groundwork for killing his father the next night. He tells Ivan that Dmitri knows Grushenka's secret knock purportedly because he is worried about Fyodor Pavlovich, but really because he wants suspicion to be cast on Dmitri so that Dmitri will be blamed when Fyodor Pavlovich's body is found. He warns Ivan about his fear of an impending epileptic seizure ostensibly as proof of his fear for Fyodor Pavlovich, but really because he wants to prepare his own alibi for the night of the murder. After all, if he is a bedridden epileptic incapacitated in the aftermath of a seizure, he is hardly capable of a murder. But as we see in Chapter 7, Smerdyakov is capable of faking a seizure so convincingly that everyone around him is fooled. These chapters are thus full of foreshadowing, as every detail—from Grigory's habit of taking a narcotic medicine to Ivan's impending departure for Moscow—sets the scene for, and builds tension toward, Fyodor Pavlovich's death.

The complex combination of disgust and attraction that characterizes Ivan's relationship with Smerdyakov manifests both Ivan's hatred of human nature and his dissatisfaction with his own philosophy. When Ivan discusses philosophy with Smerdyakov, the conflicting forces in his character become clear. Ivan is excited at Smerdyakov's interest, disgusted with Smerdyakov's manner, and unhappy with himself for providing a hostile figure like Smerdyakov with an amoral philosophy that might justify anything Smerdyakov wants to do. Smerdyakov's ingratiating behavior toward Ivan results from his realization that Ivan loathes Fyodor Pavlovich. He believes that Ivan is, on an unconscious level, using him to kill Fyodor Pavlovich. He thinks Ivan is preparing him by giving him a new moral outlook in which, because God does not play a role, there is no good or evil, and taking a life is not morally different from saving one.

Ivan's influence on Smerdyakov presents the philosophical difficulty in determining guilt for a crime. Ivan's repeated insistence that people are not responsible for one another suggests that he is morally and psychologically free of guilt for Smerdyakov's actions, no matter how much influence he may have exerted. On the one hand, if Ivan really believes everything he says about the absence of good and evil and the meaninglessness of responsibility, then he should have no cause to feel guilty about Fyodor Pavlovich's death. On the other hand, if he does not really believe in his own argument, then the complicity he exhibits here will force him to confront the fact that he is partially to blame for the murder of his hated father. Dostoevsky does not show us the outcome of this philosophical question in these chapters, but Zosima has insisted that all people are responsible for the sins of all other people, and Ivan has insisted just the opposite.

BOOK VI: THE RUSSIAN MONK, CHAPTERS 1–3

> *Obedience, fasting, and prayer are laughed at, yet they alone constitute the way to real and true freedom....*
> *(See QUOTATIONS, p. 77)*

SUMMARY — CHAPTER 1: THE ELDER ZOSIMA AND HIS VISITORS

When Alyosha returns to the monastery, he finds Zosima sitting in bed with a group of his students and followers around him. Zosima asks how Dmitri is doing and tells Alyosha that he bowed to Dmitri as he did because he foresees that Dmitri will soon undergo a great trial of pain and suffering. Zosima says that Dmitri's destiny is not Alyosha's, and encourages Alyosha again to leave the monastery and do good in the world.

SUMMARY — CHAPTER 2: FROM THE LIFE OF THE HIEROMONK AND ELDER ZOSIMA, DEPARTED IN GOD, COMPOSED FROM HIS OWN WORDS BY ALEXEI FYODOROVICH KARAMAZOV

Zosima says that he holds Alyosha very dear to his heart because Alyosha reminds him of his older brother, who was a great spiritual influence on him. Zosima's brother was a critic of religion until he came down with consumption at the age of seventeen, at which point he underwent a powerful spiritual change. In the months before he died, he talked continually about loving God's creation and all living things.

Zosima says that, in addition to his brother, the greatest influence on his life has been the Bible. But he did not discover the Bible until he was a grown man. In fact, he was a military officer, rather like Dmitri. When the woman Zosima loved married another man, Zosima challenged him to a duel and planned to kill him. But when he woke up on the morning of the duel, he saw the beauty of the world and remembered his brother's commandment to love all living things. He did not back out of the duel, however. Instead, he allowed the other man to take the first shot, and then fell to his knees and began to beg for his forgiveness. Zosima quickly left the army and decided to become a monk.

Zosima tells of one night in the past when he received a mysterious visitor, a prominent philanthropist. After asking Zosima about his conversion, and after paying him several more visits, the philanthropist confesses a great crime. He says that he once killed a woman he loved, and another man was arrested for the crime. The man who was arrested died before his trial, and the philanthropist was free. But he tells Zosima that, despite his success in life and his loving family, he has never been satisfied, because he has always longed to make a confession. Zosima encourages him to confess to the people, and after a great deal of soul-searching, the man agrees. He holds a huge birthday party, and, in front of all his guests, reads a statement of guilt. But no one believes him. It is decided that he has gone mad. Soon after, the man falls ill, and Zosima visits him at his deathbed. There, the man tells Zosima that he almost killed Zosima after he confessed his crime. But God, he says, defeated the devil in his heart. A week later, the man died, and Zosima has kept his secret until now.

SUMMARY — CHAPTER 3: FROM TALKS AND HOMILIES OF THE ELDER ZOSIMA

Zosima tells Alyosha about the importance of monks in Russian life. He says that the monk is closer to the common people than anyone else, and that the faith of the common people is the hope of Russia. He says that all people are equal in spirit, and that all people should be meek with one another, so that there are no more masters and servants.

Like his brother before him, Zosima urges all who hear him to love all mankind and all of God's creation. He says that no one should judge anyone else, even criminals. Instead, people should pray for the salvation of the wayward, to save them from spiritual hell. Zosima lowers himself to the floor, and, reaching out his arms as though to embrace the world, he dies.

ANALYSIS — BOOK VI: THE RUSSIAN MONK, CHAPTERS 1–3

The main philosophical conflict of the novel is apparent in the structural division between Books V and VI: the dark and brooding Book V is consumed with the tremors of Ivan's doubt, while the more peaceful Book VI is devoted to the quiet wisdom of Zosima's faith. Zosima's final anecdotes work as a cooling antidote to the disturbing arguments in Book V, replacing Ivan's frenzied logical examinations with more positive examples of the power of faith to do good in the world. In a way, the anecdote of the murderer is the exact opposite of the Grand Inquisitor story. The Grand Inquisitor story tells about an innocent man who is imprisoned and judged, while Zosima's anecdote of the murderer tells about a guilty man who is goes free and is forgiven. The contrast in the two anecdotes reveals a great deal about the contrast between Zosima's philosophy and Ivan's. Zosima emphasizes the power of love to overcome sin, whereas Ivan emphasizes only the baseness of the world and the cold logic with which he believes it must be faced.

In addition to the parallel between the story of the Grand Inquisitor and the anecdote of the murderer, there are a number of other parallels between things Zosima describes in Book VI and events that take place in the larger narrative, both before and after this section of the novel. For instance, Zosima's description of himself in youth as a soldier like Dmitri, with a brother who helped to redeem him spiritually, echoes the relationship between Dmitri and Alyosha: Alyosha also helps to redeem Dmitri, and Zosima says specifically that Alyosha reminds him of his brother. Zosima's youthful duel and the murder committed in the anecdote of the murderer are both crimes of passion committed for a woman's love, and thus echo the rivalry between Fyodor Pavlovich and Dmitri for Grushenka. The murderer's acceptance of responsibility and his desire to confess involve many of the same issues of responsibility and redemption that affect Ivan. These parallels ultimately are another sign of the infallible wisdom of Zosima. He is able to predict, better than anyone else, what lies ahead for the Karamazovs, and he is thus able to tailor his final lesson to what he knows will be Alyosha's needs in the coming crisis. Alyosha has proved himself capable of internalizing Zosima's lessons, and he emerges from this final conversation with Zosima better prepared to handle the hardships that lie ahead.

Zosima's death, as he stretches out his arms to embrace the Earth, is a symbol of acceptance and faith, indicating his love of God's creation with the last energy left in his body. Zosima's sincerity and his assent to the will of God are total. He does not die with fear, resentment, or regret. His final gesture is one of rapturous acquiescence, and thus Zosima's death works as an emblem of everything he has taught, spoken, and stood for throughout the novel.

Book VII: Alyosha, Chapters 1–4

Summary—Chapter 1: The Odor of Corruption
Most people within the monastery share Alyosha's feeling that a great miracle will follow Zosima's death. After Zosima's body is prepared for burial, a large crowd gathers around it in anticipation of witnessing this hoped-for divine display. But rather than dazzling onlookers with a miracle, Zosima's corpse merely exudes a putrid

stench as it quickly begins to decay. The monks are aghast, and many believe the stench to be an evil omen for the monastery.

Zosima's enemies within the monastery rudely insist that this omen indicates that Zosima was morally flawed, not a saint but an evildoer in disguise. The people in the town who had breathlessly awaited a miracle are disgruntled and confused by this disparaging talk about the widely adored Zosima. Alyosha is frightened and disgusted, and he cannot understand why God would allow this humiliation to happen.

Zosima's greatest enemy, the harsh and pious Ferapont, madly attempts to exorcise Zosima's cell of demons. He is ordered to leave the monastery, but unease reigns among the monks. Alyosha leaves as well, hoping to think things through in a quieter place.

SUMMARY—CHAPTER 2: AN OPPORTUNE MOMENT

Alyosha thinks bitterly about the degradation suffered by his beloved teacher after death. He struggles not to doubt God, but his faith in God's goodness is shaken. He simply cannot understand why a benevolent God would allow such a good man to come to such a vulgar end.

Alyosha's snide friend, the seminary student Rakitin, sees Alyosha walking and teases him about his unhappiness. He offers Alyosha sausage and vodka, morsels that monks are forbidden to consume because it is Lent, and to his surprise, Alyosha accepts them. He then asks Alyosha if he would like to visit Grushenka, and Alyosha impulsively agrees.

SUMMARY—CHAPTER 3: AN ONION

The beginning of the chapter tells Grushenka's history. Four years previously, when she is eighteen, Grushenka is brought to the town by a merchant named Samsonov and taken in by a widow. It is rumored at the time that she has been betrayed by a lover and has given her affections to Samsonov in order to win his protection. Scarcely looked after by the widow, she grows into a beautiful young woman, and, by shrewdly investing the small amount of money she has, amasses an impressive fortune in a short time. She is, and continues to be, pursued by many men in the town, but so far, none of them has succeeded in winning her.

Alyosha and Rakitin find Grushenka waiting not for them, but for a message she is expecting. She says that her former lover, an officer who abandoned her years ago, now wants her back, and she is waiting for his instructions. Excited and nervous, she jests lightly with her guests, teasing Alyosha for his purity and Rakitin for his prickly pride. Seeing that Alyosha is unhappy, Grushenka teases him by sitting on his knee. But when she hears that Zosima has died, and sees the depth and sincerity of Alyosha's grief, she suddenly sobers and becomes sad. She begins to criticize herself, calling herself a terrible sinner, but Alyosha interrupts her with kind words.

Alyosha and Grushenka suddenly feel a wave of trust and understanding pass between them. While Rakitin watches, increasingly confused and annoyed by the rapport between Grushenka and Alyosha, the latter two have a deep and rapturous conversation about their lives. Alyosha makes Grushenka feel unashamed to be who she is, and Grushenka restores Alyosha's sense of hope and faith following Zosima's death. Alyosha admits to Grushenka that, when he chose to come see her, he hoped in his despair to find a sinful woman. Grushenka admits that she paid Rakitin to bring him to her. At last the message from her lover arrives, and Grushenka leaves to join him. She asks Alyosha to tell Dmitri that she did briefly love him.

SUMMARY — CHAPTER 4: CANA OF GALILEE
Alyosha returns to the monastery and goes to Zosima's cell. There, listening to another monk reading from the Bible, he falls asleep and dreams that he is with Christ at the wedding in Cana. Zosima is also there, and he tells Alyosha to be happy. He says that Alyosha has helped to redeem Grushenka and that the young woman will now find her salvation.

Alyosha wakes with a deep joy welling in his heart. He goes outside, falls to his knees, and begins to kiss the earth. He feels as though he has come to a deeper understanding of life, faith, and God.

ANALYSIS: BOOK VII: ALYOSHA, CHAPTERS 1–4
The panic in the monastery over the stench exuded by Zosima's corpse is less bizarre than it may first appear. For modern readers, the idea of a corpse emitting a bad smell as it begins to decay is only natural. But in the lore of ancient monasteries, as in ancient medicine, odor was considered an extremely important and revealing quality. The Renaissance physician Paul Zacchias, whose 1557 work *Quaestiones medico-legales* was at the cutting edge of medical knowledge for its time, wrote that poison, infection, and disease were all transmittable through smell: "We have a thousand and one examples of living beings that have been infected by olfaction alone. . . . We see many people every day who fall into a serious or very serious state because of good or bad odors." The way something smelled, then, was deeply revealing of its inner quality.

A bad smell could be proof that something was internally diseased or corrupted. The importance of smell explains why Zosima's enemies within the monastery go into such a frenzy when Zosima's corpse begins to stink. They take the stench itself as proof of an inner unworthiness on Zosima's part, so that the smell of his corpse threatens to invalidate the wisdom of his teaching.

Additionally, the stench drives many of Zosima's followers into despair, especially those who consider him nearly a saint. In monastic legend, from the medieval era through at least the eighteenth century, the smell of a corpse is often connected to the saintliness of the soul that inhabited it so that a corpse that does not stink is a miraculous sign of the authenticity and goodness of the recently deceased person. The Jesuit historian Michel de Certeau wrote, "In innumerable stories from the convents, you can tell whether the object seen in a vision is authentic by the smell it gives off, or whether a deceased religious is a saint by the good odor surrounding her." *The Brothers Karamazov* is set in an era far removed, in some respects, from the medieval superstitions that underlie these legends—Ivan, for instance, would certainly scoff at them. But within the monastery, in a cloister in a small town in a remote part of Russia, it seems that the legends are more enduring. The high hopes that most of Zosima's followers have for a miracle following his death are dashed by the smell of his corpse, which, because of the monks' superstitions about odor, implies not only that Zosima was not a saint, but that he may not even have been a good man.

In the Grand Inquisitor chapter, we see how Christ rejects the Devil's temptation to throw himself off the pinnacle, seek salvation from the angels, and show the people below a miracle that would restore their faith. The Grand Inquisitor's insistence that Christ made a mistake in refusing to show the people a miracle is based on his emphatic belief that free will is not enough for most people to find salvation through faith: the monks illustrate this general principle that people need to witness miracles, because they are too weak to hold onto their faith without them. Everyone, even Alyosha, is optimistic about the possibility of a miracle after Zosima's death, and the speedy putrefaction of Zosima's corpse is an unpleasant reminder that, in the real world, there are no dazzling miracles, and faith is something that must be achieved without evidence.

In these chapters, Dostoevsky creates a powerful and disturbing symbol of the problem of free will in religious belief. Without the security of miracles, people are left to their own devices, to choose either faith or doubt. The choice to doubt or disbelieve can be based on a model of rational evidence, but the choice to believe must be more mystical, based on a positive feeling of meaning and profundity that is often at odds with the world as we usually experience it. Zosima's corpse represents a worldly impediment to faith. The physical reality of the world stubbornly works against the claims of faith, giving believers no validation for their belief. Even Alyosha, whose veneration of Zosima continually strengthens and protects his own faith, is driven to doubt by the events surrounding Zosima's death. The anger that he feels toward God is similar to the cold, intellectual fury that underlies Ivan's entire project of doubt. Both men are angry about God's injustice: Alyosha because God permits the posthumous humiliation of his beloved Zosima, and Ivan because God permits the suffering of children.

Rakitin and Grushenka first conspire to bring Alyosha to Grushenka's because they are threatened by his apparently unshakable purity. Their mistrust and self-doubt are manifest in Rakitin's smirking cynicism and Grushenka's angry pride. They want to upset, frighten, or corrupt Alyosha so that his own faith no longer threatens their shared belief that the world is corrupt, painful, and ugly. When the opposite happens, and Alyosha's troubled goodness elicits a chord of feeling and sympathy in Grushenka, the two young people each find unexpected salvation in their sudden understanding of one another. For Grushenka, finding a man who cares about her renews her faith in the world. Alyosha's experience with Grushenka, on the other hand, reminds him that the validation of faith lies not in miracles, but in good deeds. He believes that faith is not invalidated simply because a corpse develops a stench, but that it can be validated by active love of mankind.

Alyosha's dream of Zosima demonstrates that Zosima's legacy has not died with his body, but lives on in Alyosha's good deeds, in the forgiveness and love that are the cornerstones of his faith. Alyosha's kissing of the earth after he wakes up is a turning point for him. A deliberate echo of Zosima's final act before dying, it signifies that Alyosha has stepped into Zosima's shoes and is now fully committed to leaving the monastery and doing good in the world.

BOOK VIII: MITYA, CHAPTERS 1–8

SUMMARY — CHAPTER 1: KUZMA SAMSONOV

Dmitri is desperate for money. Even if he could persuade Grushenka to marry him, he would still be bound to repay the 3,000 rubles he owes Katerina first. But he is unable to obtain from his father the money he believes to be rightfully his, and he has no real income. In a last-ditch effort to raise the funds he needs, he visits Samsonov and attempts to strike a deal with him. He says that if the old merchant will give him the money, Dmitri will give him the rights to some land that he might be able to win from his father in court. Samsonov has no interest in this shabby deal, and cruelly attempts to dupe Dmitri. He suggests that the young man visit a different merchant to sell his land—a merchant who, unbeknownst to Dmitri, is even now planning to buy this same property from Fyodor Pavlovich.

SUMMARY—CHAPTER 2: LYAGAVY

Dmitri travels to the merchant's town, pawning his watch to pay for the transportation, but finds the man drunk. When the man has not sobered up the next day, Dmitri returns to town, desperate and uncertain of how to proceed.

SUMMARY—CHAPTER 3: GOLD MINES

Dmitri asks Madame Khokhlakov to lend him the money, but she refuses and suggests that he should go to work in the gold mines instead. He runs into Grushenka's servant and finds out that she is not at home. The servant refuses to tell him where she has gone.

SUMMARY—CHAPTER 4: IN THE DARK

Enraged, Dmitri takes a brass pestle—a small club-shaped tool used for grinding powder—to use as a weapon and hurries to Fyodor Pavlovich's house, certain that Grushenka has gone to be with his father. But when he spies through the window, he sees that Fyodor Pavlovich is alone, and when he taps out Grushenka's secret signal, Fyodor Pavlovich rushes to the window. Dmitri concludes that Grushenka is not with his father.

Grigory happens by at this moment and sees Dmitri sneaking around in the garden. He accosts him, and the men scuffle. Dmitri hits Grigory with the pestle, and Grigory falls to the ground, blood pooling beneath him. Dmitri, in a panic, tries to tend the wound, staining his clothes in the process. But then he throws the pestle into the darkness and flees the scene.

SUMMARY—CHAPTER 5: A SUDDEN DECISION

Dmitri storms back to Grushenka's house and forces the servants to tell him where Grushenka has gone. When he hears that she has joined her former lover, he is devastated. He realizes that she will never be his. Thinking that his life is meaningless without Grushenka, he decides to visit her one last time and then kill himself.

Ten minutes later, Dmitri visits Perkhotin, a local official who, earlier that day, had taken Dmitri's pistols as collateral for a ten-ruble loan. To the official's astonishment, Dmitri now displays a large amount of cash, repays the loan, and takes his pistols back. Perkhotin follows Dmitri to a store, where, to Perkhotin's continuing puzzlement, Dmitri buys several hundred rubles' worth of food and wine. Perkhotin quizzically wonders what is happening. He asks himself where Dmitri got such a large amount of money and why Dmitri is covered with blood.

SUMMARY—CHAPTER 6: HERE I COME!
Dmitri leaves Perkhotin and travels to the place where Grushenka and her lover, a Polish officer, are staying. Dmitri is in a frenzy, and raves to the coachman who drives him that he knows he will go to hell, but that, from the depths of hell, he will continue to love and praise God.

SUMMARY—CHAPTER 7: THE FORMER AND INDISPUTABLE ONE
Dmitri's arrival is awkward and his presence is unwanted by the lovers. But the scene has evidently been somewhat awkward between the lovers before his arrival, and the wine and food he brings help to lift everyone's spirits. The young people play cards.

SUMMARY—CHAPTER 8: DELIRIUM
As Grushenka watches her Polish lover cheat at the games, and listens to the coarse and degrading things that he says, she realizes she does not love him. Instead, she loves Dmitri. When the officer insults her, Dmitri attacks him and locks him in another room. Dmitri and Grushenka begin to plan their future together. Through his joy at winning Grushenka, Dmitri is troubled by the thought of the wound he dealt Grigory and the fortune he owes Katerina.

Just then, a group of officers bursts into the room. They seize Dmitri and place him under arrest. Fyodor Pavlovich Karamazov has been murdered, and Dmitri is the prime suspect.

ANALYSIS—BOOK VIII: MITYA, CHAPTERS 1–8
Dostoevsky uses a variety of literary techniques to suggest that Dmitri is responsible for his father's murder. Before Dmitri appears with a large amount of money, the narrator continually makes statements implying that Dmitri will steal Fyodor Pavlovich's 3,000 rubles: "Only three or four hours before a certain incident, of which I will speak below, Mitya did not have a kopeck, and pawned his dearest possession for ten roubles, whereas three hours later he suddenly had thou-

sands in his hands . . . but I anticipate." Dmitri's inner monologue is similarly misleading, as when Dmitri thinks about going to Madame Khokhlakov's and realizes "fully and now with mathematical clarity that this was his last hope, that if this should fall through, there was nothing left in the world but 'to kill and rob someone for the three thousand, and that's all. . . .'" Dostoevsky also uses a technique called *ellipsis,* skipping over a moment of action in order to play on our expectations: he implies Dmitri's guilt by leaving out the crucial stretch of action in Chapter 5, in between Dmitri's discovery of Grushenka's whereabouts and his arrival at Perkhotin's office. This strategy leads us to suspect that Dmitri has killed his father in that time. Finally, the events we do see suggest Dmitri's guilt. Dmitri is desperate, impassioned, and antagonistic toward Grigory. The combination of these factors makes Dmitri seem eminently capable of committing murder.

The narrative throughout this book lays the groundwork for a surprise plot twist: the revelation in Book XI that Smerdyakov, and not Dmitri, is the murderer. Dostoevsky goes to such lengths to imply that an innocent man is guilty of such a crime for several reasons. First, making Dmitri guilty and then innocent in our mind is a way of enacting the spiritual rebirth that Dmitri experiences after his arrest. Second, making us learn that our judgment about Dmitri is wrong is a way of emphasizing Zosima's advice never to judge anyone because all people are responsible for one another's sins. Third, making Dmitri appear guilty is a way of emphasizing the extraordinary scope of his passion. Dmitri may not have committed murder, but he is clearly capable of such a crime, and possesses a tormented and sinful soul. The redemption of such a passionate person is all the more dramatic. Fourth, making Dmitri appear guilty is a way of making us feel the way most of the other characters do when they learn about the arrest. The whole town believes him to be guilty.

Making Dmitri appear guilty is also a way for Dostoevsky to put human nature itself on trial. Throughout the novel we have seen various conceptions of human nature, ranging from Alyosha's faith that people are essentially good, like Zosima, to Ivan's belief that people are essentially bad, like Fyodor Pavlovich. But Dmitri combines the qualities of Fyodor Pavlovich and Zosima: he is a lustful and sinful man who nevertheless powerfully loves God. He commits bad deeds and longs to redeem them. He believes that he is bound for hell but pledges to love God even from the depths of hell. After spending a large amount of his fiancée's money on a lavish vacation with another woman, he is now greedily desperate for even more money, but only so that he can salvage his honor with Katerina, and thus make up for his sin. By putting Dmitri on trial through circumstantial evidence, Dostoevsky essentially poses the question of whether Dmitri's sinfulness or his goodness is the more fundamental aspect of his nature. This query in turn should make us question which of the two aspects is more fundamentally a characteristic of humanity. Dostoevsky wants us to consider whether humanity, burdened as it is with free will, is capable of overcoming its sinful nature and choosing to live within its good nature. When Dmitri is proved to be innocent shortly after he undergoes his powerful spiritual conversion, the question is answered in favor of human goodness—though not without a thorough understanding of the reality of evil in human life.

Although a great deal of the novel's thematic development relies on the events in these chapters, the chapters are so devoted to narrative action that there is comparatively little thematic development within Book VIII itself. Apart from the insight it offers into Dmitri's tormented inner conflict, the most interesting psychological aspect of this section is its look at Grushenka's growth since her encounter with Alyosha. Before, Grushenka is too proud and suspicious to acknowledge her love for Dmitri, but through Alyosha she discovers real goodness. As a result, she is at last capable of admitting to herself that the Polish officer is just a vulgar man who betrayed her in her youth, and that Dmitri is the man she really loves. Alyosha does not appear at all in the action of this book, but his presence is strongly felt in Grushenka's positive acquiescence to her love for Dmitri—a lovely moment of goodness that is interrupted sharply by evil, with the arrival of the police and the announcement of the murder of Fyodor Pavlovich.

BOOK IX: THE PRELIMINARY INVESTIGATION, CHAPTERS 1–9

SUMMARY—CHAPTER 1: THE START OF THE OFFICIAL PERKHOTIN'S CAREER

After Dmitri leaves Perkhotin, the official is naturally suspicious. He wonders how Dmitri got his hands on such a large amount of money, when he had been so obviously broke just hours before. Perkhotin snoops after Dmitri, learning about the brass pestle from Grushenka's maid. Then, rather than going to Fyodor Pavlovich's, he goes to Madame Khokhlakov's house, where he learns that Madame Khokhlakov refused to give Dmitri a loan. Perkhotin remembers that Fyodor Pavlovich has kept 3,000 rubles on hand in his attempt to seduce Grushenka, and he suddenly worries that Dmitri has stolen the money from his father.

SUMMARY — CHAPTER 2: THE ALARM

Perkhotin goes to tell the police about his fear, but he finds that the station is already a hubbub of activity. Grigory's wife has made another report to the police. Fyodor Pavlovich has been murdered.

SUMMARY — CHAPTER 3: THE SOUL'S JOURNEY THROUGH TORMENTS. THE FIRST TORMENT

Suspicion immediately falls on Dmitri, and he is quickly arrested. Dmitri protests his innocence, but no one believes him. Grushenka vows that she loves him despite his crime and even says that she is to blame for having deliberately toyed with both Dmitri's and Fyodor Pavlovich's affections.

SUMMARY — CHAPTER 4: THE SECOND TORMENT

Dmitri pleads innocent, but he cannot deny any of the circumstantial evidence that confronts him. He hated his father and knew about his father's 3,000 rubles. He also owed that same sum to Katerina, and took the brass pestle from Grushenka's. Finally, he traveled to his father's just before the old man was murdered. The only question Dmitri refuses to answer is about the source of the cash he obtained shortly after leaving his father's estate.

SUMMARY — CHAPTER 5: THE THIRD TORMENT

The officers continue to question Dmitri and to explore the evidence against him, trying to decide whether to charge him formally or set him free. Convinced that the truth is his ally, Dmitri seems to try to answer their questions honestly, but his evasions about the money continue to make him appear suspicious.

SUMMARY — CHAPTER 6: THE PROSECUTOR CATCHES MITYA

The officers search Dmitri's clothes and find that they are stained with blood. After the officers take his clothing as evidence, Dmitri becomes enraged with the prosecutors, and at last confesses the source of the money.

SUMMARY — CHAPTER 7: MITYA'S GREAT SECRET. MET WITH HISSES

Dmitri says that when he borrowed the 3,000 rubles from Katerina, he only spent 1,500 rubles on Grushenka. He wore the other 1,500 in a locket around his neck. But once he decided to kill himself, he decided there was no reason to hold onto the 1,500 rubles, so he spent some of it on wine and food for his last meeting with Grushenka.

SUMMARY—CHAPTER 8: THE EVIDENCE OF THE WITNESSES. THE WEE ONE
The problem is that Dmitri has always told people that he spent the entire 3,000 rubles on Grushenka, and the prosecution is now able to produce several witnesses who say that he told them he needed the full 3,000 rubles to repay Katerina.

SUMMARY—CHAPTER 9: MITYA IS TAKEN AWAY
Grushenka is called in to testify. Dmitri swears to her that he did not kill his father, and she believes him. But the officers nevertheless decide to keep him in prison to await a trial. Dmitri says good-bye to Grushenka, asking her to forgive him for everything he has done. Grushenka delivers an impassioned promise to love and remain loyal to Dmitri forever.

ANALYSIS—BOOK IX: THE PRELIMINARY INVESTIGATION, CHAPTERS 1–9
This book is devoted to a description of the circumstantial evidence that makes Dmitri appear guilty of Fyodor Pavlovich's murder. The question of whether Dmitri is guilty symbolically represents the greater question of whether human nature is fundamentally good or sinful, so the legal proceedings against Dmitri represent the trial of the human spirit. Just as Book V, especially in the Grand Inquisitor chapter, presents the novel's indictment of God, Book IX begins its indictment of humanity. This book recounts Dmitri's past in detail, and the stories of his innumerable sins are retold, as though to summarize the moral failings that lie at the heart of the case. Dmitri has lied to everyone, stolen from and cheated Katerina, turned to violence against Grigory, and been unable to control his passions for Grushenka. In short, he has committed the most common and universal sins of mankind.

Dmitri's bizarre, almost gleeful reaction to this list of sins reveals the seeds of his redemption. In Zosima's anecdote of the murder in Book VI, Dostoevsky has drawn our attention to a peculiar psychological phenomenon: the desire of a guilty man to confess his guilt. The murderer in this anecdote had gotten away with his crime, but he could never find happiness because he was desperate to confess his guilt. As Zosima indicates in his argument with Ivan over ecclesiastical courts in Book II, conscience is the sternest judge of all. Even a criminal who has gotten away with his crime can be judged by his conscience. Like the murderer in Zosima's anecdote, Dmitri has a conscience that judges him harshly, and also like the murderer, Dmitri is guilty, not of the charge of killing his father, but of all the lies, acts of violence, and other sins of his past. Like the murderer, part of Dmitri longs for his crimes to be known and judged, so he can find redemption in the suffering of his punishment. Dmitri's glee throughout this passage is due in part to Grushenka's declaration of love for him. But he also experiences relief to be in the hands of the police and to hear his crimes discussed openly and critically. This review of his past sins may seem like a damning indictment of humanity, but it is actually the first step in Dmitri's transformation from a tormented and sinful man into a faithful and loving one.

BOOK X: BOYS, CHAPTERS 1–7

SUMMARY — CHAPTER 1: KOLYA KRASOTKIN

It is the beginning of November—a dull, cold day just before the start of Dmitri's trial. Kolya Krasotkin is a thirteen-year-old boy who was once a friend of Ilyusha. Kolya loves dogs and likes to train his dog, Perezvon, to do tricks. Kolya is two years older than Ilyusha, and has a somewhat blustery and impertinent nature. He appears to be conceited, but he is actually a loyal friend, and likes looking out for children younger than himself.

SUMMARY — CHAPTER 2: KIDS

At present, Kolya is watching two children while their mother, a tenant of his mother, is away. He is anxious, however, because he wants to go visit Ilyusha. Ilyusha has fallen ill and may be near death. Alyosha has convinced the other boys to visit him every day, but Kolya has yet to visit him once. He has not met Alyosha yet either.

SUMMARY — CHAPTER 3: A SCHOOLBOY

At last, a servant returns to the house, and Kolya hurries to Ilyusha's house with Perezvon in tow.

Outside Ilyusha's house, Kolya meets his friend Smurov, who is disappointed that he brought Perezvon. Smurov says that the other boys were hoping he would bring Zuchka, a dog that Ilyusha has apparently been desperate to see. Kolya contemptuously declares that he does not know where Zuchka is, and he asks Smurov to send Alyosha out to him before he goes in to see Ilyusha.

SUMMARY—CHAPTER 4: ZUCHKA

Alyosha comes out to meet Kolya, impressing him immediately by speaking to him as an adult and not talking down to him. As they speak, Kolya is increasingly taken with Alyosha's unself-conscious wisdom and his unaffected manner of speech. Kolya tells Alyosha about his history with Ilyusha. He says that when the other boys used to pick on Ilyusha, Kolya was impressed by the fact that Ilyusha always fought back bravely, even thought he was undersized. Kolya eventually decided to protect Ilyusha, and they became good friends. But Ilyusha sometimes resented Kolya's influence over him and sometimes did things out of spite just to rebel against Kolya. Once, for instance, Ilyusha performed a cruel trick some of the boys had learned from Smerdyakov—feeding a dog a piece of bread with a pin hidden in it. Kolya, enraged, tried to punish Ilyusha. In the ensuing scuffle, Ilyusha stabbed Kolya with a knife, thus ending their friendship, though Kolya says he does not hold a grudge. The injured dog was named Zuchka, and no one seems to know whether it lived or died. Alyosha tells Kolya that Ilyusha believes his illness was caused by God's wrath over his treatment of Zuchka.

SUMMARY—CHAPTER 5: AT ILYUSHA'S BEDSIDE

Alyosha and Kolya go inside, where Kolya impresses Ilyusha's mother by bowing to her. The pale and bedridden Ilyusha is thrilled to see Kolya, but all the boys around the bed are disappointed that he was unable to bring Zuchka. Kolya mocks Ilyusha about Zuchka, asking how any dog could possibly have survived eating a pin for an appetizer. Then, he calls for Perezvon, and when Perezvon runs into the room, Ilyusha cries out that it is Zuchka. Kolya did find Zuchka, and then gave the dog a different name so that no one would spoil his surprise for Ilyusha.

Katerina, still guilty over Dmitri's beating of Ilyusha's father, has summoned a doctor from Moscow to look after the boy, and when he arrives, Ilyusha's guests are forced to leave.

SUMMARY—CHAPTER 6: PRECOCITY

Outside the house, Alyosha and Kolya talk, and Kolya tells Alyosha his views on life, which he is certain are both profound and final despite the fact that he is only thirteen years old. Alyosha sees at once that Kolya's "philosophy" is merely a batch of phrases and modern ideas he has heard from Rakitin. But he listens respectfully, and when he disagrees with what Kolya says, he says so, and says why. Even though Alyosha says Kolya's sweet nature has been perverted by Rakitin, Kolya is still so drawn to Alyosha that he feels they have become close friends. Alyosha agrees and inwardly hopes that Rakitin's influence will not have a permanent effect on this young self-proclaimed socialist.

SUMMARY—CHAPTER 7: ILYUSHA

The doctor leaves, and Alyosha and Kolya both realize that Ilyusha will soon die. Ilyusha speaks softly to his father about his death, and Kolya, who has been choking back tears at the sight of his sick friend, at last begins to weep openly. He tells Alyosha that he will come to visit Ilyusha as often as he can, and Alyosha admonishes him to keep his word.

ANALYSIS

The stories of Alyosha's influence on Kolya, Ilyusha, and the other boys develop a motif of the novel: the idea that faith and virtue can be taught and handed down as a legacy from one faithful man to the next. This legacy begins with Zosima's brother, who teaches Zosima about loving God's creation and forgiving mankind. Zosima passes the lessons on to Alyosha, and Alyosha now actively passes them on to the young boys he has befriended since his initial encounter with Ilyusha, keeping the chain of faith alive. Dostoevsky dramatizes the receptivity of children to moral teachings throughout this section of the novel. If Alyosha's example is only partly successful in improving the lives of the adults to whom he is close, it is more successful among the children here in Book X. The boys look at Alyosha with unmitigated respect and adoration because he treats them with respect—as equals—as we see in his extended conversations with the wayward Kolya. *The Brothers Karamazov* ends on a note of optimism and encouragement, and a great deal of its positive tone seems to stem from the idea that Alyosha's role as a teacher of the young will improve the faith of the next generation.

This part of the novel shows Alyosha's reaction to Ivan's indictment of God. In these chapters, Alyosha encounters the very injustice that makes Ivan reject God—the suffering of children—and shows his response to it. Rather than recoiling in intellectual horror, as Ivan does, Alyosha devotes himself to doing what he can to make the suffering child happier, bringing Ilyusha's schoolmates to see him every day, helping to heal the rift between Ilyusha and Kolya, and generally providing Ilyusha and his family with friendship and support. Just as Zosima's argument with Ivan in Book I stems from their opposite perspectives, with Zosima treating other people on an individual basis and Ivan looking at mankind as a whole, the contrast between Alyosha and Ivan in this situation stems from the same opposition. Ivan looks at the abstract idea of suffering children and is unable to reconcile the idea with his rational precepts about how God ought to be. His solution is to reject God. Alyosha, on the other hand, sees an actual suffering child and believes that it is God's will for him to try to alleviate the child's suffering to whatever degree he can. His solution is to help Ilyusha. Again, Dostoevsky shows how the psychology of skepticism walls itself off, in elaborate proofs and theorems, from having a positive effect on the world, while the psychology of faith, simplistic though it may be, concerns itself with doing good for others. This very subtle response to the indictment of God presented by Ivan in Book V brings the philosophical debate of the novel onto a plane of real human action, and shows the inadequacy of Ivan's philosophy—which Ivan himself would readily acknowledge—to do good in the real world.

BOOK XI: BROTHER IVAN FYODOROVICH, CHAPTERS 1–10

But hesitation, anxiety, the struggle between belief and disbelief—all that is sometimes such a torment for a conscientious man like yourself, that it's better to hang oneself....

(See QUOTATIONS, p. 77)

SUMMARY—CHAPTER 1: AT GRUSHENKA'S
On a wintry day almost two months after Dmitri's arrest, Alyosha travels to visit Grushenka. Alyosha and Grushenka have grown closer since Dmitri's arrest, and are now close friends. Grushenka fell ill three days after the arrest, but is now almost fully recovered. As her friendship with Alyosha has deepened, Grushenka has begun to show signs of spiritual redemption as well. Her fiery temper and her pride are still intact, but her eyes now shine with a new light of gentleness. She tells Alyosha that she and Dmitri have had an argument, and that she fears that Dmitri is in love with Katerina again, even though Katerina has not once visited him in prison. Grushenka also believes that Dmitri and Ivan are hiding something from her. She asks Alyosha to find out what it is, and Alyosha agrees to do so.

SUMMARY—CHAPTER 2: AN AILING LITTLE FOOT
Before Alyosha speaks to Dmitri, he must pay a visit to Madame Khokhlakov and Lise. Madame Khokhlakov speaks to him before he sees Lise, and tells him something very curious: Ivan has recently paid a visit to Lise, after which Lise's already erratic moods have become even

more unbalanced. Madame Khokhlakov asks Alyosha to find out what is troubling Lise and to tell her after he has found out.

SUMMARY — CHAPTER 3: A LITTLE DEMON

Lise is nearly hysterical when Alyosha goes in to see her. After they decided to become engaged, she changed her mind and broke off the engagement, and now, she says, she does not even respect Alyosha, because she cannot respect anyone or anything. She says that she wants to die because the world is so loathsome. She describes speaking to a "certain man" about this subject and says that the man laughed at her and left. She asks if the man despised her, and Alyosha says that he did not. As Alyosha rises to leave, Lise gives him a note for Ivan. When Alyosha is gone, she slams her finger in the door, crushing her fingernail. As she looks down at the blackened, bloody nail, she whispers to herself that she is mean.

SUMMARY — CHAPTER 4: A HYMN AND A SECRET

Alyosha goes to the prison, where Rakitin has just visited Dmitri. Perplexed, Alyosha asks Dmitri about the visit, and Dmitri says Rakitin wants to write an article alleging that, because of his circumstances, Dmitri could not have helped but kill his father. Dmitri says he holds Rakitin in contempt, but allows him to visit so he can laugh at his ideas. Sobering, Dmitri tells Alyosha that even though he is not guilty of the crime of which he is accused, he has come to terms with the burden of sin he has created for himself and longs to do penance and redeem himself. He is only afraid that Grushenka will not be allowed to travel with him to his exile in Siberia, and that without her, he will lack the strength necessary for his spiritual renewal.

Dmitri says that Ivan has recently offered him a plan for his escape, even though Ivan believes Dmitri to be guilty of the murder. This plan is the secret that they have been keeping from Grushenka. Tormented with grief and guilt, Dmitri refuses to escape before the trial. He asks Alyosha what he believes, and Alyosha says that he has never believed Dmitri to be guilty. This declaration from his younger brother fills Dmitri with courage and hope.

SUMMARY — CHAPTER 5: NOT YOU! NOT YOU!

Alyosha finds Ivan outside Katerina's. Ivan tells him that Katerina has a letter from Dmitri that proves he is the murderer. Alyosha does not believe it. He insists that Dmitri is innocent. Ivan asks cuttingly who the murderer could be, if it is not Dmitri. Alyosha says that Ivan obviously considers himself indirectly responsible for the crime, and Alyosha reassures him that he is not. He says that God has sent him to soothe Ivan's conscience. Ivan is troubled by Alyosha's religiosity and storms away.

SUMMARY — CHAPTER 6: THE FIRST MEETING WITH SMERDYAKOV

Since the murder, Smerdyakov has been sick and is now near death. Ivan has visited him twice, and now goes to see him again. During their first visit, Smerdyakov asserts that Ivan left his father on the day of the murder because he suspected his brother Dmitri would kill their father, and Ivan secretly wanted their father to die.

SUMMARY — CHAPTER 7: THE SECOND VISIT TO SMERDYAKOV

During Ivan's second visit, Smerdyakov says that he believes Ivan wished Fyodor Pavlovich to die so that he would inherit a large portion of his wealth. After this visit, Ivan is suddenly forced to accept that he bears part of the blame for the murder. He goes to visit Katerina, and she shows him a letter in which Dmitri promises to kill Fyodor Pavlovich if necessary to repay her 3,000 rubles. This reassures Ivan that Dmitri is responsible for the murder, and that he himself bears no responsibility for it.

SUMMARY — CHAPTER 8: THE THIRD AND LAST MEETING WITH SMERDYAKOV

On Ivan's third visit to Smerdyakov, Smerdyakov openly confesses that he murdered Fyodor Pavlovich. But he says that he could not have done so had his philosophical discussions with Ivan not given him a new understanding of morality that made it possible for him to kill. For this reason, he says, Ivan is as much to blame for the murder as Smerdyakov is.

SUMMARY — CHAPTER 9: THE DEVIL. IVAN FYODOROVICH'S NIGHTMARE

Ivan returns home, thinking that he will now be able to prove Dmitri's innocence at the trial tomorrow. But in his room, he has a nightmarish hallucination or vision: a luridly dressed middle-aged man who claims to be a devil. The devil taunts Ivan about his doubt and insecurity, and though Ivan is harshly critical of the devil, the apparition eventually drives him mad.

SUMMARY — CHAPTER 10: "HE SAID THAT!"

At last Alyosha knocks at the door, and the devil disappears. Ivan insists that what happened was real, but he is hysterical and seems to be undergoing a mental collapse. Before realizing that Ivan is having a nervous break-down, Alyosha tells him his news: Smerdyakov has hung himself and is dead. Alyosha spends the night caring for Ivan and praying for him.

ANALYSIS — BOOK XI: BROTHER IVAN FYODOROVICH,
CHAPTERS 1–10

Lise's miserable behavior makes her a parody of Ivan. Like Ivan, she is frustrated and hurt by the world's injustice, saying that she cannot respect anything. But whereas Ivan reacts to his frustration with an intellectually rigorous despair, Lise merely allows her doubts, both about the world and herself, to overwhelm her, so that she loses the ability to take anything seriously. Ivan's laughter at Lise's expression of her emotions is a response that involves both pity and contempt. One of the main ideas of *The Brothers Karamazov* is that suffering can bring salvation, and that people who purge their sins through suffering can attain self-knowledge and redemption. Grushenka goes through this process, with Alyosha's aid, in the aftermath of her horrible illness. But Lise vulgarizes this notion: her slamming the door on her finger is a pathetic attempt to invoke this principle, but because her attempt to suffer is full of such obvious vanity and self-pity, it is only a mockery of the lofty idea it seeks to copy.

Apart from Zosima, Alyosha is the most moral character in the novel, and the strength and clarity of his faith are the moral center of the novel. For Alyosha to have faith in Dmitri is not surprising, because Alyosha has faith in human nature. On the other hand, there is a sense in which, within the scope of the novel, the great philosophical conflicts that run through the story are all riding on the question of Dmitri's guilt or innocence. Thus, if Alyosha places his faith in Dmitri and is proved wrong, the idea of faith will be thrown into doubt.

Ivan's collapse into madness at the end of this section demolishes his cold dignity and reveals the terrifying emptiness at the heart of his philosophy. At the same time, his crisis brings some of the central ideas of the novel into direct conflict. As the novel progresses, Ivan continually resists the notion that he bears any moral responsibility for the actions of other human beings, saying instead that people are only responsible for their own actions. But his conversations with Smerdyakov gradually illustrate for him the role he played in enabling Smerdyakov to murder Fyodor Pavlovich. Ivan is therefore forced to accept the universal burden of sin for the first time, and it is the agony of this burden that leads to his mental breakdown. In a sense, Ivan's skepticism is fueled by his general distrust of humanity.

He withdraws into his detached intellectualism in part because he is unable to love other people, and wants to remain separate from them. Smerdyakov's revelation that Ivan's philosophy enabled him to murder Fyodor Pavlovich finally makes clear to Ivan the extent to which people are involved in one another's lives. While illuminating the terrifying consequences of Ivan's amoralism, Smerdyakov's crime also shatters the walls Ivan has built around himself, and, in a way, the rest of humanity comes flooding in on him. Without the consolation of faith, Ivan cannot handle this burden. His hallucination of the devil, like the revelation of Smerdyakov's guilt, shows him the nature of a world without God, but having so thoroughly rejected God, Ivan is left defenseless. His breakdown results from the collision between the psychology of doubt and the idea of moral responsibility. Ivan could endure one. He cannot endure both.

Smerdyakov's motivations for killing Fyodor Pavlovich are vague. Smerdyakov believes Ivan wanted him to kill Fyodor Pavlovich. But he has other motivations as well. Smerdyakov may be living Ivan's philosophy that if there is no God, all is permitted. He may also kill for the money, or out of his own hatred of Fyodor Pavlovich. Finally, Smerdyakov may simply feel a desire to do evil. Allegorically, the murder signifies the logical extreme of Ivan's arguments. Smerdyakov shares Fyodor Pavlovich's brutish wickedness, and so, in a sense, Fyodor Pavlovich is killed by his own loathsome way of living. Ivan's conviction that good and evil are fraudulent categories, and that no one has any moral responsibility to anyone else, has facilitated the destruction of one amoral monstrosity by another. The deeply moral Ivan loses his mind when confronted with the horror of this development, as apparently does Smerdyakov, whose unmourned suicide is the final cry of terror and pain to come from the novel's exploration of the nihilism of disbelief.

BOOK XII: A JUDICIAL ERROR, CHAPTERS 1–14

SUMMARY — CHAPTER 1: THE FATAL DAY

Dmitri's trial opens at ten o'clock the next morning, amid an atmosphere of widespread curiosity. All Russia seems to be interested in the outcome, and the legendary defense attorney Fetyukovich has traveled all the way from Moscow to defend Dmitri. The judge is known to be an educated man, but the jury is made up of peasants, leading to some concern that Fetyukovich's defense will be above the heads of the jury members.

The judge asks Dmitri for his plea, and he again asserts his innocence. The general consensus in the courtroom, given what most people consider to be overwhelming evidence, is that he is guilty.

SUMMARY — CHAPTER 2: DANGEROUS WITNESSES
A sequence of witnesses is called, and one by one, through masterful cross-examinations, Fetyukovich casts suspicion on their words, discrediting their claims that Dmitri is guilty. Grigory, Fetyukovich notes, had taken a strong medicine on the night of the murder, and his senses may have been unreliable.

SUMMARY — CHAPTER 3: MEDICAL EXPERTISE
Three doctors offer contradicting theories about what might have led Dmitri to commit the murder, and about the condition of his mind. One doctor, a German who has lived in the town for many years, tells a story about buying Dmitri a bag of nuts when he was a little boy. Dmitri weeps, evoking a new sympathy in the minds of his listeners.

SUMMARY — CHAPTER 4: FORTUNE SMILES ON MITYA
Alyosha next offers some useful evidence: he remembers that Dmitri used to hit the locket on his chest in moments of self-loathing, implying that perhaps he really was wearing the money around his neck, and did not steal it from Fyodor Pavlovich. Alyosha also admits that he believes Smerdyakov may be the real murderer.

Katerina tells the story of Dmitri saving her father from prison. The crowd, which was impressed with Alyosha's testimony, is slightly disgusted with Katerina because she has so thoroughly debased herself before Dmitri, who does not love her. Grushenka is questioned and vehemently insists on Dmitri's innocence.

SUMMARY — CHAPTER 5: A SUDDEN CATASTROPHE
The next witness called is Ivan, who has been suffering from an illness that has made him nearly insane. Ivan rages and rambles, asserting that Smerdyakov killed their father. He shows the courtroom a wad of cash, which he says Smerdyakov stole from Fyodor Pavlovich. He says that he himself is also to blame, because he knew that Smerdyakov would kill Fyodor Pavlovich, and did not stop him. He says that the man who knows the truth of what he says is the devil, who visits him at night. As he becomes more and more intense and animated, he is finally removed from the courtroom.

Katerina, to defend Ivan's honor, reverses her earlier testimony, showing the court the letter Dmitri sent her in which he said that he might kill his father. She says that Ivan has lost his sanity out of grief for his brother's guilt, and that he only claims responsibility for the murder to take the blame from Dmitri. Grushenka furiously flings insults at Katerina, and the courtroom dissolves into chaos.

SUMMARY—CHAPTER 6: THE PROSECUTOR'S SPEECH. CHARACTERIZATIONS
When order is restored, the lawyers give their closing speeches. The prosecutor, Kirrillovich, runs down the facts of the case.

SUMMARY—CHAPTER 7: A HISTORICAL SURVEY
Kirrillovich says that Dmitri has the temperament of a man who would be capable of such a violent act, and that he is not insane.

SUMMARY—CHAPTER 8: A TREATISE ON SMERDYAKOV
Kirrillovich says that unlike Smerdyakov, Dmitri had a motive to kill Fyodor Pavlovich because he hated the old man and craved his money. Given the violent sentiment of the letter Dmitri wrote to Katerina, Kirrillovich says, his guilt seems clear.

SUMMARY—CHAPTER 9: PSYCHOLOGY AT FULL STEAM. THE GALLOPING TROIKA. THE FINALE OF THE PROSECUTOR'S SPEECH
Kirrillovich exhorts the jury to punish Dmitri to defend the cause of justice in Russia, and to annihilate the perpetrator of the most hateful crime imaginable—the murder of a father by a son.

SUMMARY—CHAPTER 10: THE DEFENSE ATTORNEY'S SPEECH. A STICK WITH TWO ENDS
Fetyukovich counters by pointing out the flimsiness of all the evidence against Dmitri. Apart from circumstance and the conjecture of unreliable witnesses, there is no proof that Dmitri is guilty.

SUMMARY—CHAPTER 11: THERE WAS NO MONEY. THERE WAS NO ROBBERY
Fetyukovich continues his summation. He points out that there is not even any proof that Fyodor Pavlovich kept an envelope full of 3,000 rubles; it is only a rumor. The letter that Dmitri wrote to Katerina was written drunkenly and under extreme emotional torment, and cannot be taken as a statement of Dmitri's real intention.

SUMMARY—CHAPTER 12: NO MURDER EITHER
Finally, Fetyukovich says, even if Dmitri had killed Fyodor Pavlovich, he would not have been murdering his father, because the repug-

nant old man never acted as his father and forgot about the boy the moment he was born.

SUMMARY—CHAPTER 13: AN ADULTERER OF THOUGHT

Fetyukovich insists that Dmitri's only chance to find redemption amid the tattered shreds of his life is to be set free.

SUMMARY—CHAPTER 14: OUR PEASANTS STOOD UP FOR THEMSELVES

Most of the crowd has been completely won over to Dmitri's side. Everyone expects that he will be set free. But the jury returns in a short time and declares that Dmitri is guilty. The crowd is outraged. Dmitri cries out that he is innocent and that he forgives Katerina. Grushenka cries out from the balcony, and Dmitri is led away.

ANALYSIS—BOOK XII: A JUDICIAL ERROR, CHAPTERS 1–14

Dmitri's trial in Book XII is in many ways an anticlimax. Book XI contains a more shocking sequence of events, including Smerdyakov's confession, Dmitri's spiritual redemption, Ivan's mental collapse, and Smerdyakov's suicide. These revelations resolve the novel's pressing moral questions, establish Dmitri's innocence, and make whatever happens in the courtroom less consequential to the novel's larger themes. In Book XII, Dostoevsky satirizes the Russian legal system through the incredibly long, pompous closing speeches of the lawyers. Part of the novel's premise, however, is that the real judgment of Dmitri's soul could not possibly take place in a courtroom. The idea that no human judgment can supplant the judgment of one's own conscience first appears in Book I, when Zosima argues against Ivan's proposals for the ecclesiastical courts by pointing out that no court could hope to judge a man as he must judge himself.

Crime and justice are important motifs in *The Brothers Karamazov,* and the trial is the most sustained look at criminal justice in the novel. Dostoevsky refrains from pushing analytical conclusions about the nature or quality of Russian jurisprudence, and instead chooses simply to offer a thorough depiction of how a Russian criminal trial might actually look: he emphasizes the styles of legal argumentation, ranging from Fetyukovich's precise dissections of witness's statements to the rougher and more direct style of Kirrillovich; the emotions of the witnesses; and, above all, the reaction of the crowd to the drama at hand.

Dostoevsky's decision to write much of Book XII from the perspective of the crowd as a whole is both philosophically and aesthetically significant. This perspective gives the novel a sense of completion by providing dramatic resolution in both its individualistic and its abstract modes. The conflict has been played out between the two perspectives on humanity represented by Zosima and Ivan, the one looking at people as individuals, the other looking at humanity as an abstract whole. In Book XI, with the total collapse of Ivan's philosophy, Dostoevsky gives us the private, individual resolution of the novel's great questions, the most important resolution and the one matching Zosima's worldview. In Book XII, he provides the large-scale, abstract resolution of the same questions from the perspective of the mob. The crowd comes to believe in Dmitri because they are moved by his story, suggesting that human nature is more good than it is evil. The crowd's final reversal of their original impression that Dmitri is guilty—so that everyone in the room thinks he is innocent except the jurors—is Dostoevsky's encouraging testament to mankind's ability to discover truth. The crowd challenges the cynical assessment of mankind offered by Ivan and the Grand Inquisitor, even if it does so by allowing itself to be moved by the emotional drama of Dmitri's story.

EPILOGUE, CHAPTERS 1–3

SUMMARY—CHAPTER 1: PLANS TO SAVE MITYA

Katerina has brought the raving Ivan back to her house, and Alyosha visits them there after the trial. Katerina is torn with regret over her betrayal of Dmitri at the trial, but she says an ironclad plan is in place for his escape. In order to free him, however, Alyosha will have to play a part. Alyosha agrees to do whatever is necessary to secure Dmitri's freedom.

SUMMARY—CHAPTER 2: FOR A MOMENT THE LIE BECAME THE TRUTH

Alyosha visits Dmitri in prison and tells him about the plan for his escape. Though Dmitri longs to be redeemed by suffering, and has, in a sense, accepted the idea of his punishment, he agrees to the escape plan so that he will be able to remain with Grushenka. He will have to flee to America, but he says he will not spend his entire life away from Russia. One day, he will return.

Katerina arrives. She and Dmitri reconcile, and Katerina tells him that she never truly believed him to be guilty. Grushenka arrives, and when Katerina begs for her forgiveness as well, Grushenka refuses to forgive her. Katerina runs from the room. Dmitri reproaches Grushenka, and Alyosha tells him sternly that he has no right to be critical of her. Alyosha then runs after Katerina. She says that she cannot blame Grushenka for not forgiving her.

Summary — Chapter 3: Ilyushechka's Funeral. The Speech at the Stone

Ilyusha is dead, and Alyosha must now attend his funeral. He discusses Dmitri's case with Kolya and some of Ilyusha's other friends. He asks them earnestly always to hang on to the feeling of closeness, love, and companionship that they now share. The crowd of schoolboys cheers Alyosha adoringly.

Analysis — Epilogue, Chapters 1–3

The epilogue of the novel discusses the redemption of the main characters. The first part of the novel's short epilogue completes the redemption of Katerina, which begins at the trial when she cries out to save Ivan. In bringing Ivan back to her house to recover from his illness, Katerina has finally become capable of seeking her own happiness in the world honestly and without choosing to suffer merely to point out the guilt of those who make her suffer. She and Dmitri are now fully capable of forgiving one another because they have both been purged of the sins that have plagued them for so long. Though Dmitri has not lost the desire to repent for his sins through suffering—a desire very different from Katerina's urge to suffer in order to draw attention to the sins of others—he is willing to accept the escape plan because he has come to the mature realization that there is more to goodness and faith than suffering. His spirit will be stronger if he can be with Grushenka. Grushenka's inability to forgive Katerina shows that her own redemption is incomplete. She is still proud, but, as Alyosha realizes when he scolds Dmitri for criticizing her, she is on the right path.

The novel ends, paradoxically, on notes of warmth, hope, and optimism in the middle of a funeral. Alyosha's words to the schoolboys again emphasize his influence with children and the promise that influence holds for the future. As in Book X, Alyosha emerges as a natural teacher, capable of continuing Zosima's legacy of faith, love, and forgiveness throughout his life. The novel's last words are very hopeful: Kolya leads the schoolboys in chanting, "Hurrah for Karamazov!" The use of the family surname is significant here, since throughout the novel, characters have discussed "the Karamazov quality" and "the Karamazov legacy" as being defined by Fyodor Pavlovich's violence, uncontrolled passion, and lust. The final words of the novel imply that the Karamazov legacy has changed: it is no longer defined by Fyodor Pavlovich, but by Alyosha. The Karamazov family has been redeemed.

Important Quotations Explained

1. "Above all, do not lie to yourself. A man who lies to himself and listens to his own lie comes to a point where he does not discern any truth either in himself or anywhere around him, and thus falls into disrespect towards himself and others. Not respecting anyone, he ceases to love, and having no love, he gives himself up to the passions and coarse pleasures, in order to occupy and amuse himself, and in his vices reaches complete bestiality, and it all comes from lying continually to others and to himself."

Zosima makes this speech to Fyodor Pavlovich in Book II, Chapter 2. Many of Zosima's comments in this section of the novel lay the groundwork for the development of the novel's main ideas. Here, Zosima explores the important concept that the path to virtue is through honesty with oneself. A man who lies to himself, he says, is unable to perceive the truth around him. Because his surroundings make him suspicious, and because he cannot believe in anything—not God, not other people—he ceases to respect or to love mankind and thus falls into sin. This argument is not only a perceptive summary of Fyodor Pavlovich's psychology, it also opens the door for many of the novel's subsequent ideas about redemption. Later, the novel suggests that the path to redemption lies in honest self-knowledge, which can best be attained through suffering.

2. "Listen: if everyone must suffer, in order to buy eternal harmony with their suffering, pray tell me what have children got to do with it? It's quite incomprehensible why they should have to suffer, and why they should buy harmony with their suffering."

Ivan makes this argument to Alyosha in Book V, Chapter 4, as part of his rejection of the idea of a loving God. Ivan believes it is impossible to have faith in a benevolent deity who makes children suffer unjustly. Ivan can, to a certain extent, see the logic in the suffering of adults: adults must suffer to pay for their sins, "to buy eternal harmony with their suffering." But children, he explains, are too young to have sinned, and are often made to suffer the most excruciating torments by a God who supposedly loves them. From this condition, Ivan reasons that if God exists, he does not really love mankind, but rather occupies the position of a torturer who should be defied and rejected rather than worshipped and loved.

3.   "Decide yourself who was right: you or the one who questioned you then? Recall the first question; its meaning, though not literally, was this: 'You want to go into the world, and you are going empty-handed, with some promise of freedom, which they in their simplicity and innate lawlessness cannot even comprehend, which they dread and fear—for nothing has ever been more insufferable for man and for human society than freedom! But do you see these stones in this bare, scorching desert? Turn them into bread and mankind will run after you like sheep, grateful and obedient, though eternally trembling lest you withdraw your hand and your loaves cease for them.'"

The Grand Inquisitor levels this accusation at Christ in Ivan's prose poem in Book V, Chapter 5. The inquisitor is referring to the story of the temptations that Satan offered Christ, and that Christ rejected. The Grand Inquisitor sees Christ's rejection of the temptations of Satan as responsible for placing the intolerable burden of free will on mankind, and for taking away the comfort of stability and security. The Inquisitor says that when Satan tempted Christ to make bread from the stones, Christ should have done so, and should have brought the bread back to the people so that they would follow him in order to win the security of being fed. Christ's response—that man does not live by bread, but by the word of God—gives men the freedom to choose whether to follow Christ or not, without buying faith with security. This notion of free spiritual will is central to Christian theology, but as the Grand Inquisitor sees it, Christ has actually done mankind a disservice by keeping people from obtaining security. Most people, he says, are too weak to tolerate the burden of free will. As a result, he says that "the one who questioned you then," meaning Satan, was right, and Christ was wrong. Ivan believes that mankind is not competent to handle the awesome burden of free will, and should have been given a leader to obey instead.

4. "Very different is the monastic way. Obedience, fasting, and
    prayer are laughed at, yet they alone constitute the way to
    real and true freedom: I cut away my superfluous and
    unnecessary needs, through obedience I humble and chasten
    my vain and proud will, and thereby, with God's help, attain
    freedom of spirit, and with that, spiritual rejoicing!"

Zosima makes this speech when analyzing the nature of the Russian
monk in Book VI, Chapter 3. It illustrates the scope of the contrast
between Zosima's views and Ivan's. Where Ivan's Grand Inquisitor
looks at the problem of free will with resentment and loathing, Zosima
considers free will a cause for rejoicing. The Grand Inquisitor says that
men should have been given bread and leadership, while Zosima says
that they should reject material security—through obedience, fasting,
and prayer—in order to obtain "real and true freedom." For Zosima,
real and true freedom is crucial to the nature of goodness because it
gives meaning to the choice to embrace faith. If a person has no choice
but to believe in God, then faith is meaningless—only through the
medium of free will can faith be more than a default position. Zosima
thus wholly rejects the Grand Inquisitor's—and Ivan's—notion of the
weakness of human nature, holding out hope that, through spiritual
freedom, mankind can be redeemed.

5. "But hesitation, anxiety, the struggle between belief and
    disbelief—all that is sometimes such a torment for a
    conscientious man like yourself, that it's better to hang
    oneself. . . . I'm leading you alternately between belief and
    disbelief, and I have my own purpose in doing so. A new
    method, sir: when you've completely lost faith in me, then
    you'll immediately start convincing me to my face that I am
    not a dream but a reality—I know you know; and then my
    goal will be achieved. And it is a noble goal. I will sow a just
    a tiny seed of faith in you, and from it an oak will grow—
    and such an oak that you, sitting in that oak, will want to
    join 'the desert fathers and the blameless women'; because
    secretly you want that ver-ry, ver-ry much. . . ."

This taunt is delivered by the devil that visits Ivan in Book XI, Chapter
9. Ivan has just realized his complicity in Smerdyakov's murder of Fyodor Pavlovich, and in his ensuing psychological breakdown, he experiences the hallucination of this devil, who mocks Ivan with his former

beliefs and their inconsistency with his inner desires. Ivan furiously tries to assert that he does not believe this devil is real, but the devil shrewdly manipulates his desire not to believe so as to make him believe all the more. Then, in this passage, the devil even more shrewdly admits that he is deliberately toying with Ivan's belief because he knows that deep down Ivan wants to believe in him. Ivan is a moral person who is horrified and appalled by the rejection of morality that he advocates on the surface, and the murder of his father has made him even more desperate in his secret desire for the moral criterion of religious faith. This inner longing makes Ivan ashamed, and the devil teases his shame, even assuming a mockingly singsong tone of voice ("ver-ry much, ver-ry much"). This passage is important because it strips Ivan's psyche bare and reveals the emotional emptiness and desperation that lie beneath his philosophical positions. Ivan's doubt collapses into a nervous breakdown, revealing, through his hallucination of the devil, both the inadequacy of his doubt and his secret desire to find a more satisfying faith.

KEY FACTS

FULL TITLE
  The Brothers Karamazov

AUTHOR
  Fyodor Dostoevsky

TYPE OF WORK
  Novel

GENRE
  Realist novel; novel of ideas; symbolic novel;
  dynastic novel

LANGUAGE
  Russian

TIME AND PLACE WRITTEN
  1879-1880; Russia, primarily St. Petersburg

DATE OF FIRST PUBLICATION
  1879–1880

PUBLISHER
  The Russian Messenger began publishing the novel serially in
  1879.

NARRATOR
  An unnamed, first-person narrator who acts as a storyteller,
  relating events in which he plays no part. The narrator frequently
  refers to himself as "I," and his erratic voice leaves a noticeable
  sardonic mark on an otherwise serious novel.

POINT OF VIEW
  The point of view shifts between characters, including Alyosha,
  Ivan, Dmitri, and the
  narrator himself.

TONE
  The narrator's tone is one of serious comedy. He takes his story
  seriously and comprehends the importance of the questions it
  raises, but nevertheless writes with a warm linguistic
  inventiveness that sometimes masks the coldness of his subject.

TENSE
Past

SETTING (TIME)
Mid-nineteenth century

SETTING (PLACE)
A town in Russia

PROTAGONIST
Alyosha Karamazov

MAJOR CONFLICT
Dmitri and Fyodor Pavlovich's rivalry over Grushenka, Ivan's inner turmoil, and Alyosha's good-hearted attempts to help those he loves find happiness dramatize the philosophical conflict between religious faith and doubt.

RISING ACTION
Fyodor Pavlovich and Dmitri begin to fight over the family inheritance just before Alyosha's faith is shaken by the death of Zosima. Ivan expresses his philosophical viewpoint through the story of the Grand Inquisitor, and Dmitri becomes increasingly desperate to win Grushenka.

CLIMAX
Ivan's nervous breakdown in Book XI after the revelation that Smerdyakov is the murderer represents the final collapse of the psychology of doubt and the moment at which the position of faith seems inarguably superior, at least within the logic of the novel.

FALLING ACTION
Dmitri is wrongly convicted of murdering his father, and Dmitri and Katerina reconcile their differences. Alyosha's final speech to the schoolboys at the funeral of Ilyusha illustrates that he has taken on the role of Zosima.

THEMES
The conflict between faith and doubt; the pervasiveness of moral responsibility; the burden of free will

MOTIFS
Crime and justice; the profound gesture; redemption through suffering

SYMBOLS

Characters who represent ideas, as Ivan represents doubt; Zosima's corpse

FORESHADOWING

The narrator's many leading comments; Zosima's prediction that Dmitri will suffer greatly; the anecdote of the murderer in Zosima's deathbed speech; Smerdyakov's subtle clues that he intends either to have Dmitri murder Fyodor Pavlovich or to murder Fyodor Pavlovich himself.

Study Questions & Essay Topics

Study Questions

1. *Compare and contrast Ivan's and Zosima's belief systems. How do they differ regarding the novel's major philosophical questions?*

Zosima emphasizes belief in God, love, forgiveness, and goodness, while Ivan's beliefs emphasize doubt, skepticism, and a rejection of conventional moral and religious categories. Zosima thus advocates faith as a method for finding happiness, and Ivan advocates doubt as a method for realistically interpreting the world. Their stories dramatize the emotional, psychological, and spiritual consequences of adopting the positions that they represent. Zosima lives happily and does good in the world, while Ivan lives unhappily and, through his influence on Smerdyakov, enables evil. Through the contrast between these two characters, as through many similar contrasts in the novel, Dostoevsky illustrates the superiority of faith and love over doubt and suspicion.

2. *Dostoevsky goes to great lengths to make us suspect that Dmitri is guilty of the murder of Fyodor Pavlovich. Why does it matter whether Dmitri is innocent or guilty? Why might Dostoevsky have wanted to surprise us with his innocence?*

Because it is frequently difficult to decide whether Dmitri is on the side of goodness or of sin, Dmitri's situation in the novel is representative of the human situation as a whole. The novel questions the moral orientation of human nature by asking whether mankind is fundamentally good and innocent, or evil and guilty. Because Dmitri represents the human situation as a whole, the question of his guilt or innocence assumes titanic importance in the novel. If Dmitri is guilty, then, in a sense, mankind is guilty, and the novel will end in despair. But if Dmitri is innocent, there is still hope, and the novel can end optimistically. There are many reasons why Dostoevsky may have wanted us to suspect Dmitri's guilt, including the simple dramatic power of a surprise twist in the plot. But the primary reason may be that by making us first perceive Dmitri to be guilty and then realize that he is innocent, Dostoevsky wants to make us undergo a conversion in our conception of Dmitri at the same time that Dmitri himself is undergoing a spiritual conversion. This process creates a powerful visceral sense that Dmitri has been washed clean of his sin. The revelation of Dmitri's innocence reinforces the emotional power of his conversion.

3.   *How can Fyodor Pavlovich's coarse, pleasure-seeking behavior be understood as a logical expression of the philosophy advocated by Ivan? What does Ivan's reaction to Fyodor Pavlovich's lifestyle say about the sincerity of Ivan's beliefs?*

Ivan believes that human morality depends on the idea that the soul is immortal. Therefore, the only reason people have to be good is to ensure their future happiness in the afterlife. Because Ivan rejects the notion that the soul is immortal, he also rejects the categories of good and evil, and claims that all is permitted—that is, that people may do anything they choose without reference to moral restrictions on their behavior. Of all the characters in the novel, Fyodor Pavlovich most fully embodies this idea. He seeks only to satisfy his own appetites, without regard for good or evil, without regard for religion, and without regard for what other people might think of him. In this way, Fyodor Pavlovich's lifestyle represents a logical extension of Ivan's philosophy. But rather than embracing Fyodor Pavlovich's amoral approach to life, Ivan recoils in disgust. Because of his beliefs, he is not able to reject Fyodor Pavlovich outright, but though he pretends to accept the old man, he really loathes him and is consumed with self-disgust at the thought that his philosophy renders him unable to reject Fyodor Pavlovich's way of life. In this way, we see that Ivan's beliefs, though compelling, are not entirely sincere. He believes in them because they appear to be rational, but as his confrontation with the devil after Fyodor Pavlovich's murder proves, he does not accept them with his whole heart.

QUESTIONS & ESSAYS

SUGGESTED ESSAY TOPICS

1. *The Brothers Karamazov places a great deal of emphasis on the idea of free will—the idea that faith has meaning because each person is free to choose between faith and doubt. But though many of the novel's major characters struggle with doubt, Alyosha, the protagonist, often seems to have such an instinctive faith that he could never choose to be faithful because he simply is. Does the concept of free will apply to a character such as Alyosha? Why or why not?*

2. *Think about the many mysterious symbolic gestures made by religious figures throughout the novel—Christ kissing the Grand Inquisitor, for instance, or Zosima bowing before Dmitri. Do these profound gestures, meant to articulate ineffable aspects of religious belief, represent a logical argument against the philosophy of doubt, or do they constitute a different order of expression entirely?*

3. *Compare and contrast the novel's principal female characters, Grushenka and Katerina. In what way does the concept of redemption apply to each of them, and how do they each go about finding the redemption that they seek? How different are their situations—morally, socially, psychologically—from those of the other main characters, simply by virtue of their being women?*

4. *Explain the idea of moral legacies within the novel—the notion that a system of moral teachings can be passed down from one person to the next, as Zosima passes his beliefs to Alyosha. Within this context, what is the significance of Alyosha's relationship with the schoolboys in Book X and the Epilogue?*

5. *What are Smerdyakov's traits as a character? What are his apparent philosophical beliefs? Does he really believe the lessons he claims to have learned from Ivan, or does he merely use Ivan's philosophy to justify his own murderous desires?*

REVIEW & RESOURCES

QUIZ

1. What is the verdict at Dmitri's trial?

    A. Guilty
    B. Innocent
    C. A mistrial is declared
    D. Dmitri never comes to trial

2. Which of the Karamazov brothers does Miusov help to raise?

    A.   Ivan
    B. Alyosha
    C. Dmitri
    D. Smerdyakov

3. Which character is the son of Stinking Lizaveta?

    A. Ivan
    B. Smerdyakov
    C. Dmitri
    D. Alyosha

4. Why does Dmitri leave Katerina?

    A. He wishes to become a monk
    B. He is in love with Marfa
    C. He knows that Katerina loves Ivan
    D. He is in love with Grushenka

5. To whom does Alyosha become engaged?

    A. Lise
    B. Katerina
    C. Grushenka
    D. Madame Khokhlakov

6. What does Fyodor Pavlovich offer Grushenka if she chooses
   him over Dmitri?

   A. His undying love and respect
   B. A farm in the Balkans
   C. His finest horse
   D. 3,000 rubles in cash

7. Who tells Dmitri about Grushenka's secret knock?

   A. Ivan
   B. Smerdyakov
   C. Ilyusha
   D. Katerina

8. What does Kolya claim as his political affiliation?

   A. Revolutionary liberalism
   B. Communism
   C. Monarchism
   D. Socialism

9. Who brings Zuchka to Ilyusha's bedside?

   A. Kolya
   B. Alyosha
   C. Ilyusha's father
   D. No one

10. How does Christ respond to the Grand Inquisitor's list of
    accusations?

    A. He begins to weep
    B. He turns away from the Grand Inquisitor
    C. He kisses the Grand Inquisitor on the lips
    D. He kneels before the Grand Inquisitor

11. What is the subject of Dmitri's hallucination?

    A. Satan
    B. A minor devil
    C. Katerina
    D. Jesus

12. Which elder is Alyosha's teacher?

    A. Ferapont
    B. Paisy
    C. Miusov
    D. Zosima

13. What single injustice troubles Ivan most?

    A. The suffering of children
    B. Poverty and starvation
    C. The exaltation of evil men
    D. Bad things happening to good people

14. Who raises Smerdyakov?

    A. Fyodor Pavlovich
    B. Alyosha
    C. Grigory and his wife
    D. Samsonov

15. Who introduces Alyosha to Grushenka?

    A. Samsonov
    B. Rakitin
    C. Dmitri
    D. Katerina

16. Who exhibits the letter at Dmitri's trial?

    A. Grigory
    B. Fyodor Pavlovich
    C. Kirrillovich
    D. Katerina

17. Who slams her own hand in the door?

    A. Madame Khokhlakov
    B. Lise
    C. Grushenka
    D. Katerina

REVIEW & RESOURCES

18. What do the schoolboys chant after Alyosha's speech at the funeral?

    A.   "Hurray!"
    B.   "Hurrah for Alyosha!"
    C.   "Hurrah for Karamazov!"
    D.   "Hurrah for Ilyusha!"

19. When and where does the Grand Inquisitor story take place?

    A.   Sixteenth-century Spain
    B.   Present-day Russia
    C.   Mid-nineteenth-century England
    D.   Medieval France

20. Which of the following was an actual experience of Dostoevsky that influenced the writing of *The Brothers Karamazov*?

    A.   The murder of his father
    B.   His time in prison
    C.   His epilepsy
    D.   All of the above

21. Who brings Grushenka to the town?

    A.   Alyosha
    B.   Dmitri
    C.   Fyodor Pavlovich
    D.   Samsonov

22. Who asks Alyosha to leave the monastery?

    A.   Ivan and Dmitri
    B.   Zosima and Fyodor Pavlovich
    C.   Zosima alone
    D.   Dmitri alone

23. What does Madame Khokhlakov suggest when Dmitri asks her for a loan?

    A. That he sell his pistols
    B. That he take his father to court
    C. That he go to work in the gold mines
    D. That he marry Katerina for her money

24. What is the subject of Ivan's controversial essay?

    A. Ecclesiastical courts
    B. Transubstantiation
    C. The Eucharist
    D. The evils of the pope

25. Who kills Fyodor Pavlovich?

    A. Dmitri
    B. Grushenka
    C. Alyosha
    D. Smerdyakov

ANSWER KEY:

1: A; 2: C; 3: B; 4: D; 5: A; 6: C; 7: B; 8: D; 9: A; 10: C; 11: B; 12: D; 13: A; 14: C; 15: B; 16: D; 17: B; 18: C; 19: A; 20: D; 21: D; 22: B; 23: C; 24: A; 25: D

REVIEW & RESOURCES

SUGGESTIONS FOR FURTHER READING

BELKNAP, ROBERT L. *The Genesis of* THE BROTHERS KARAMAZOV: *The Aesthetics, Ideology, and Psychology of Text-Making.* Evanston, Illinois: Northwestern University Press, 1990.

———. *The Structure of The Brothers Karamazov.* The Hague and Paris: Mouton, 1967.

DOSTOEVSKY, FYODOR. *Crime and Punishment.* Translated by David McDuff. New York: Penguin Classics, 1993.

———. *The Idiot.* Translated by Alan Myers. New York: Oxford University Press, 1998.

FRANK, JOSEPH. *Dostoevsky.* Princeton, New Jersey: Princeton University Press, 1996.

MOCHULSKY, KONSTANTIN. *Dostoevsky: His Life and Work.* Princeton, New Jersey: Princeton University Press, 1967.

SUTHERLAND, STEWART R. *Atheism and the Rejection of God: Contemporary Philosophy and* THE BROTHERS KARAMAZOV. Oxford: Blackwell, 1977.

REVIEW & RESOURCES